USA TODAY®

A GANNETT COMPANY

Lifeline

TIM TEBOW
Quarterback with Conviction

by Stephen G. Gordon

Twenty-First Century Books · Minneapolis

For my buddy Ralph

Twenty-First Century Books
A division of Lerner Publishing Group, Inc.
241 First Avenue North
Minneapolis, MN 55401 U.S.A.

Website address: www.lernerbooks.com

Library of Congress Cataloging-in-Publication Data

Gordon, Stephen G.
    Tim Tebow : quarterback with conviction / by Stephen G. Gordon.
      p. cm. — (USA Today lifeline biographies)
    Includes bibliographical references and index.
    ISBN 978–1–4677–0809–8 (lib. bdg. : alk. paper)
    1. Tebow, Tim, 1987– —Juvenile literature. 2. Football players—United States—Biography—Juvenile literature. 3. Quarterbacks (Football)—United States—Biography—Juvenile literature. I. Title.
GV939.T423G67 2013
796.332092—dc23   2012018017

Manufactured in the United States of America
1 – CG – 12/31/12

Tebow takes over: Denver Broncos quarterback Tim Tebow makes a pass during a game against the Miami Dolphins in October 2011. Tebow led Denver's comeback during the 2011–2012 season.

Tebow Time

For football fans in Denver, Colorado, 2011 was looking like another bleak year. Going into the sixth game of the season, their hometown Broncos had won just one game and lost four. In 2010 the team had gone 4–12, a franchise record for losses in a single season. The once-mighty Denver Broncos, winners of two Super Bowl championships, had fallen to a new low.

Denver fans were even more frustrated because sitting on the Broncos bench was

Tim Tebow, one of the most talked-about quarterbacks in football. At the University of Florida, Tebow had been a superstar. He had taken his team to two national championships and had won the prestigious Heisman Trophy—the highest individual honor in college football. When Denver had picked Tebow in the first round of the National Football League (NFL) draft in 2010, "Tebow fever" had swept through Colorado.

But for most of 2010 and early 2011, Tebow just sat on the sidelines. Broncos fans wondered: What are the coaches waiting for? Why not give Tebow a shot? With another sorry season unfolding ahead of them, what did the Broncos have to lose? Some fans even paid to have a billboard posted on the interstate highway running through Denver. It was addressed from Broncos fans to coach John Fox. "Play Tebow," it said.

A New Game Plan

Fox had been hesitant to give Tebow much playing time. Yes, Tebow had been a star in college. Yes, he was a fan favorite. But that didn't mean he was ready to take the reins of an NFL team. Fox and the other Denver coaches had planned to play Tebow sparingly behind their starting quarterback, Kyle Orton.

Taking a chance: Denver coach John Fox put backup quarterback Tebow into the game to see what he could do on the NFL playing field.

But as the Broncos lost one game after another in early 2011, Coach Fox finally came to agree with the fans. Why not play Tebow? Kyle Orton was turning out to be a big disappointment. Fox announced that Tebow, not Orton, would start against the Miami Dolphins at an away game on October 23. Everyone hoped he could deliver a much-needed victory.

Down but Not Out

Hopes were high. But when Tebow at last took the field to start against Miami, it seemed as though he could not deliver much of anything. In fact, he could barely complete a pass. For three-plus quarters, he kept missing open receivers. The Miami defense sacked him seven times. The Miami fans hooted and jeered at Tebow as he messed up one play after another. This was the superstar Denver had been pinning its hopes on?

Time was running out. Miami was sitting on a 15–0 lead midway through the fourth quarter. The Broncos were staring into the jaws of a shutout—a game in which they didn't score at all. The team hadn't been shut out since 1992—almost twenty years before.

But five minutes were left, and a lot can happen in five minutes of football. A lot did happen. First, Tebow led his team on an 80-yard touchdown drive, bringing the score to 15–7. At that point, less than three minutes remained. Denver had to get the ball back quickly to make another score. Instead of kicking off deep into Miami territory, the Broncos took a risk with an onside kick—a short kick to give them a chance of recovering the ball. The gamble paid off. A Miami receiver bobbled the kicked ball, and Bronco Virgil Green came up with it at the Broncos' 44-yard line.

With 2:31 left on the clock, Tebow had the ball back in his hands. This time he marched his players 56 yards down the field for another touchdown. That put the score at 15–13. Without a two-point conversion—a run or completed pass from the 2-yard line into the end zone instead of the normal extra-point kick—Denver would go home with a

Running the ball: Tebow cradles the football as he runs in for the two-point conversion to tie the game against Miami.

loss. Tebow didn't want to let that happen. Taking the ball at the snap, he kept it to himself and barreled into the end zone. The score was tied 15–15.

The remaining seventeen seconds ticked off the clock, sending the game into overtime. The first team to score in overtime would win, and the Dolphins had the ball first. But they didn't have it for long. Denver's D. J. Williams sacked the Miami quarterback and forced a fumble. It was the Broncos' turn to make the game winner, which they did with a 52-yard field goal by Matt Prater.

Tebowing
As the other Denver players mobbed Prater and celebrated, Tim Tebow slipped off quietly to the sidelines, kneeled down on one knee, put

his fist to his forehead, and prayed. A deeply religious man, Tebow always prayed in this manner before and after games.

Back in Denver, fans watching on TV couldn't believe their eyes. Just when they thought another Bronco loss was certain, Tebow had come through with a stunning overtime victory. Maybe the season wasn't lost after all.

In New York City, twenty-four-year-old

A quiet moment: Tebow kneels in prayer after winning the Miami game. Fans called the pose Tebowing.

Denver native Jared Kleinstein watched the Miami game with friends in a bar. Like other Bronco fans, Kleinstein had caught Tebow fever. After watching the quarterback kneel in prayer after the game, Kleinstein and five friends decided to pay homage to Tebow. They kneeled on the sidewalk outside the bar, fists to their foreheads, and had someone take their picture.

Kleinstein posted the picture on his Facebook page. A few days later, he set up a website, Tebowing.com, and asked people to submit pictures of themselves in the Tebow pose. Immediately, photos poured in by the hundreds. Page views climbed to the hundreds of thousands.

Soon everyone from sportscasters to celebrities were "Tebowing," defined on the website as "to get down on a knee and start praying, even if everyone else around you is doing something completely

All over the world: A fan Tebows in front of Stonehenge, an ancient site in Britain.

different." Some people struck the pose because they too were religious. Others did it because they just loved football, especially Tim Tebow.

Something about Tebow had captured the imagination of people around the world—football fans and non-football fans alike. Something made him special. In the weeks and months that followed, Tim Tebow would show the world even more of his special talents.

On Mindanao: Faithful worshippers gather at a Christian chapel in the hills of Mindanao.

All in the Family

Tim Tebow calls Florida home. That's where he grew up, went to school, and learned to play football. But Tim wasn't born in Florida or even in the United States. Tim was born half a world away in the Philippines, an island nation in Southeast Asia.

Tim's parents, Bob and Pam Tebow, had met at the University of Florida in Gainesville. They married in 1971. Bob became a Christian minister in Jacksonville, Florida. He led the congregation at the

Southside Baptist Church and then at the Cornerstone Community Church.

In the early 1980s, Bob took a short trip to the Philippines to teach Filipino people about Christianity. When he came back to Jacksonville, Bob realized that his work in the Philippines was not finished. He wanted to return to preach and to set up Christian churches there.

By then the Tebows had four children, Christy, Katie, Robby, and Peter. In 1985 the whole clan packed up and moved to General Santos City on Mindanao, one of the thousands of islands that make up the Philippines. There, Bob founded the Bob Tebow Evangelistic Association (BTEA).

In 1986 the family learned that another child was on the way. Pam had a difficult pregnancy and traveled to Manila, the Philippine capital, to deliver the baby boy. He arrived on August 14, 1987. Bob and Pam named him Timothy, which means "honoring God" in ancient Greek. The family called him Timmy or Tim for short.

Bob continued his religious work, preaching and organizing churches throughout the Philippines. The children went to school, but it was not an ordinary school. Back in Florida, Pam had set up a home-school to teach the Tebow children herself. She gave the kids lessons in typical subjects such as math and reading, but she also included many lessons about God and Christianity. Pam continued homeschooling the kids in the Philippines.

Timmy was too young for school, so he just played and ran around at home with his big brothers and sisters. The older boys, Robby and Peter, especially liked to play football and baseball, and toddler Timmy tagged along after them.

"Farmer Strong"

In 1990 the family returned to Jacksonville, to the house they had left behind five years earlier. But with five growing kids, that house was just too small. So the family moved again, this time to a 44-acre (18-hectare) farm on the western outskirts of Jacksonville. Bob continued his work with the BTEA, and Pam continued to home-school the kids.

At the same time, the whole family ran the farm. They grew vegetables and raised cattle and horses. All the kids had to do farm chores. Tim and the others grew "farmer strong" by lifting hay bales, chopping wood, herding cows, and mending fences.

The Tebow boys loved playing sports. Robby was six years older than Tim, and Peter was three years older. They towered over their little brother. But Tim was a fierce competitor and kept up with his brothers in every game they played. They played basketball outside for hours. They played football in the mud.

Homeschool Days

Like his brothers and sisters, Tim attended the family homeschool. Each child worked one-on-one with Pam for part of the day. When she was giving a lesson to one child, the others read, studied, and did problems independently. Pam gave the kids homework, tests, and grades, just as a regular classroom teacher would. At the end of the

IN FOCUS

Golf on the Farm

Tim and his brothers liked to play golf. But they didn't play the traditional way, on a professionally built golf course. Instead, the boys cut down patches of grass in the pasture on their farm to create four putting greens. With a posthole digger, they cut a hole in the ground in the middle of each green. Then they enjoyed their own private four-hole golf course.

year, the kids took assessment tests designed for public school students to make sure their math, reading, and other skills were on par with those of most kids their age.

Early on, Pam realized that Tim was dyslexic. Dyslexia is a learning disability that makes it difficult for a person to make sense of written words and sentences. Both Tim's dad and his brother Robby are dyslexic too. Like other people with dyslexia, Tim learned better by doing than by reading about how to do something. Pam tailored her teaching to her son's special style of learning. If he had troubling grasping a concept or skill, she slowed down the lesson. Since Tim was the only kid in the class, he and Pam could take as much time as they needed to tackle a lesson, without worrying about Tim falling behind other students.

Some people worry that homeschoolers don't socialize enough with other children, but that wasn't the case for Tim and his sisters and brothers. In the early 1990s, Pam started an organization called First at Home, an association of homeschool families in Jacksonville. Through the association, the parent-teachers shared lessons, textbooks, and other classroom materials. The kids got together for field trips and social activities. In addition, Tim met lots of kids through church. He never felt lonely or isolated as a homeschooler.

Pam taught the kids early in the day, which left plenty of time for sports and other activities in the afternoon. But for the Tebow children, learning never really ended. Pam created placemats showing all

A closer look at prayer

The survey found 87% of Americans pray.

How often do you pray or meditate outside of religious services:

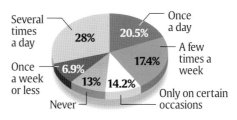

Several times a day 28%
Once a day 20.5%
A few times a week 17.4%
Once a week or less 6.9%
Never 13%
Only on certain occasions 14.2%

Source: Baylor survey

By Frank Pompa, USA TODAY, 2006

Onstage

The Tebows belonged to the First Baptist Church of Jacksonville *(right)*. They attended worship services regularly. The church also offered sports, clubs, and other activities for youngsters. The kids put on musical plays at Christmastime and in summer. In the second grade, Tim got his first part in a church musical. He and another boy wore a camel costume. Tim was the back half of the camel. After that, Tim got better roles. He played a sailor, a Supreme Court justice, and Superman. He continued acting in church productions all the way through high school.

the U.S. presidents, state and world capitals, and other facts and figures. The kids raced and quizzed one another at dinnertime to see who could master the facts on the placemats fastest. But learning at the Tebow home wasn't limited to typical school subjects. It also included a lot of religious lessons. At breakfast, the family read Bible verses. The kids had to memorize five verses each week and recite them on Saturday night.

League Play

Tim joined a Little League baseball team at the age of five. He was assigned to the T-ball division, with other kids his age. In this division, most players aren't skilled enough to hit pitched balls. Instead, they use a tee. A tee is a post that holds a ball steady, so it's easy to hit.

Since Tim played so much baseball at home, he had no problem hitting pitches. He didn't need a tee. During his at-bats, a coach pitched to him underhand. Five-year-old Tim smacked one home run after another, many of them soaring over the fence in the ballpark. After T-ball, Tim moved up to the next division in Little League, for players aged seven to eleven. He also played basketball in a church league.

When Tim was eight, he joined a Pop Warner football team in Jacksonville. Pop Warner is a kid's football league, similar to Little League baseball. Tim started out in the peewee division for younger kids. He wanted to play quarterback, but with his big, athletic build, the coaches thought he was a better fit as a running back. Tim was frustrated. Quarterback was his favorite position when he played with his brothers at home.

In his four years of Pop Warner football, Tim played quarterback for two seasons and running back for two seasons. "I hung with it to be a team player," Tim remembers about his years as a running back, "but I was chomping at the bit to play quarterback. Football was my favorite sport, but what made it fun for me was playing quarterback."

Whether at home or in league play, it was clear that Tim stood out from the crowd of young athletes. "He definitely showed talent at an early age—being able to throw the [foot]ball," recalled Tim's brother Robby. "I can remember him being in the backyard throwing the ball about forty yards." For a peewee-age football player, this distance was impressive.

When Tim was eleven, baseball coaches invited him to play for the Jacksonville Tidal Wave, made up of the city's best Little League players. The Tidal Wave went up against other top teams from around Florida and throughout the United States. The boys played a grueling schedule of ten or eleven games per week in summer, with two games each on Friday, Saturday, and Sunday. Tim played with the Tidal Wave for three seasons.

December 9, 2004

At 75, Pop Warner Football Going Strong

<u>From the Pages of</u>
<u>USA TODAY</u>

Pop Warner, a youth football program for ages 5 to 16, was established in 1929 and later renamed for legendary coach Glenn S. "Pop" Warner. Programs exist in 42 states and six foreign countries. They require participants to maintain academic standards in order to take part. According to the NFL and Pop Warner, about 70% of current NFL players started in the youth league.

—Evan Miller

Pop Warner: A youth football program, Pop Warner has a long history. Here, young players get ready to play in a championship game in 2009.

A left-hander, he was part of the team's pitching squad. But Bob Tebow kept a close eye on his youngest son's athletic activities. He believed that a pitcher—especially a young one—could burn out his throwing arm. Bob didn't want to see his son injured. He told the coach that Tim could pitch only once a week, with a maximum of eighty-five pitches per game. When he wasn't pitching, Tim played in the outfield.

Competitive Edge

Tim wanted to be the best in every sport he played. Looking to edge out the competition, he worked out and built up his muscles. Tim wanted to lift weights, but his father wouldn't allow it. Bob knew that Tim gave 110 percent to everything he did—workouts included. If Tim overdid it with weights, he might damage his bones, tendons, or muscles. So instead of weight lifting, Tim attached some rubber tubing to the top of a doorway. He pulled on the tubing, with one arm and then the other, for thirty minutes at a time. This kind of exercise, called resistance training, allowed him to strengthen his arms, chest, and shoulders without injury. Tim also included push-ups and sit-ups in his workout routine.

Finally, when Tim was around thirteen, his dad let him add weight training to his workouts. For Christmas, his parents gave him a weight set, which he kept in the barn at the farm. Early in the morning and late at night, he worked out like a madman, lifting weights and doing four hundred push-ups and four hundred sit-ups each day.

During workouts, Tim stayed focused on his number one goal: winning on the playing field. His mother remembers, "He was extremely competitive. So when people tried to tell him, it doesn't matter if you win or lose, it's just about having fun, he would just look at us so puzzled. Because to him it mattered."

"Bottom line," said Tim later, "losing simply isn't any fun."

CHAPTER TWO

At Trinity: The Main Street Bridge leads to downtown Jacksonville, Florida, where Tim played football for Trinity Christian Academy.

Front and Center

One drawback of homeschooling is that homeschools don't have sports teams. Sometimes, kids from several families attend homeschool together, but even large homeschools usually don't have enough students to form organized teams.

Many homeschoolers solve this problem by joining sports teams at private schools in their towns. The two oldest Tebow boys, Robby and Peter, played sports at Trinity Christian Academy in

Jacksonville. When Tim reached eighth grade, he followed in his brothers' footsteps. He joined the junior varsity football team at Trinity Christian. Tim played quarterback. The team went undefeated that year.

Muscle Man

Tim continued his aggressive home workouts. He packed on weight and grew taller. By the age of fourteen, Tim stood nearly 6 feet (1.8 meters) tall and weighed 175 pounds (79 kilograms). By then Robby was playing football for Carson-Newman College in Tennessee. He sent Tim the book and schedule used for his team's workouts, and Tim adopted that program. To keep up his energy and strength, he drank lots of protein shakes. He decided to cut out soft drinks for a while, because he knew all the extra sugar wasn't good for his body.

In the summer between eighth and ninth grade, Tim attended football camp in Ocala, Florida. The camp was run by three quarterbacks who played or had played in the NFL: Kerwin Bell, Shane

Getting strong: As a boy, Tim worked out to gain strength and muscle. He used resistance training *(above)* to condition his muscles. Later, he added weight lifting to his workout routine.

Matthews, and Danny Wuerffel. All of them had been quarterbacks at the University of Florida. Most of the other boys at camp were older, but Tim was named the top quarterback at the end of the program.

Tim got even more football advice from Gannon Shepherd. He had played defensive end at Duke University in North Carolina. After that, he joined the Jacksonville Jaguars. Tim's sister Katie, a sports nut like her brothers, worked for the Jaguars as an intern. She met Gannon, and they began dating. (They later married.) When Katie took Gannon home to visit her family, he and Tim often went outside and did football drills.

Freshman Funk

Football season rolled around, and Tim—by then a high school freshman—joined the Trinity varsity football team. Tim's brother Peter was also on the team. A senior, Peter was playing his last year of high school ball. Tim was excited to play on the same team as his brother. Peter played linebacker, a defensive position, and the coach wanted Tim to play linebacker too. Tim wasn't happy at linebacker. He hadn't been happy as a running back. He wanted to play quarterback.

Tim stuck out the season for his freshman year, playing linebacker and sometimes tight end. Trinity had a great season, winning the state championship for the first time in

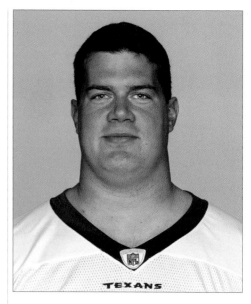

Brother-in-law: Gannon Shepherd played briefly for the NFL's Jacksonville Jaguars. He later married Tim's sister Katie.

its history. But for Tim, the season was frustrating. He played mostly on defense while another boy led the team as quarterback. When football season ended, Tim played basketball and then baseball for Trinity. He was a standout in those sports too.

Going into his sophomore year, Tim didn't want to return to Trinity. He knew he might get placed at linebacker again. But as a homeschooler, Tim wasn't really stuck with Trinity. After all, he wasn't a regular student there. He just joined the football and other sports squads for practices and games. Tim and his parents decided to move on from Trinity. They looked around for another Jacksonville-area school that might let Tim join the team at quarterback. They settled on Nease High School, which had just hired a new, highly regarded football coach, Craig Howard.

Joining Nease was a little tricky, though. It was a public school, not a private school like Trinity. The rules about homeschoolers joining public school teams in Florida were stricter than those governing homeschoolers on private school teams. To play for Nease, Tim would have to live in St. Johns County, south of Jacksonville, where Nease was located. He couldn't live on the farm. So Tim and his mom—his teacher—moved to an apartment in St. Johns County. They returned to the farm on weekends but lived in the apartment Monday through Friday.

Swooping: Tim's swooping football-throwing motion was evident when he was a quarterback at Nease High School.

February 15, 2012

Demographics Evolve among Home Schools

From the Pages of USA TODAY

There was a time when Heather Kirchner thought mothers who home-schooled their children were only the types "who wore long skirts and praised Jesus and all that."

That was before the New Jersey resident decided to home-school her own daughter, Anya.

Kirchner favors jeans, and like the two dozen other families that are part of the year-old Homeschool Village Co-op in central New Jersey, she doesn't consider herself to be particularly religious. "I was definitely not ready to hand over to anybody my 5-year-old, my baby," she says. "I would hate to miss this [Anya's education]. They grow too quickly."

The New Jersey co-op is among hundreds of secular [nonreligious] home-schooling groups in the USA aimed at providing opportunities for parents to network and for children to socialize, conduct science experiments, play sports and games and more, according to Homeschool World, the website of *Practical Homeschooling Magazine*.

Secular organizations across the country report their numbers are growing. Though government records indicate religion is still the driving force in home schooling, members of these organizations say the face of home schooling is changing, not because of faith, but because of what parents see as shortcomings in public and private schools.

Joyce Burges, who co-founded National Black Home Educators (NBHE) with her husband, Eric, says most of the parents she deals with have practical, not religious, reasons for home schooling. NBHE's network of families has seen a jump from about 500 home schoolers a decade ago to about 2,500 today, she says.

She says her area near Baton Rouge [Louisiana] has some of the lowest-scoring schools in the nation. "A lot of the children are just falling through the cracks," Burges says. Her five children, ages 16 to 35, were home-schooled, says Burges. "Parents are struggling, trying to see what they can do."

According to a home-schooling survey in 2007 by the federal government's National Center for Education Statistics, a little more than 1.5 million children in the USA were being home-schooled. That represents an increase from 1.1 million students being home-schooled in spring 2003, according to the center.

The percentage of the school-age population home-schooled increased in that period from 2.2% to 2.9%. The center will release new home-schooling statistics this fall.

The 2007 survey showed 83.3% of home-schooling parents named "a desire to provide religious or moral instruction" as an important reason to home-school.

Susan Beatty, co-founder and general manager of the Christian Home Educators Association of California, who home-schooled three now-grown children, says most of her group's members are looking to offer "a distinctly Christian education."

A Home School Legal Defense Association study in 2009 by the National Home Education Research Institute showed home schoolers, on average, scored 37 percentile points above public school students on standardized achievement tests. "Parents are disgusted with the school system," [homeschool association founder Norma] Curry says. "The majority, they're just looking for something better."

—Alesha Williams Boyd

Homeschool: Elizabeth Boggs works with her two sons on a geography lesson in their home. Boggs and her family are part of a network of homeschoolers in Charleston, Illinois.

Quarterback at Last

In the fall of 2003, Tim Tebow and Craig Howard—new quarterback and new coach—had their work cut out for them. The year before, the Nease High football team had won only two games. The team's veteran players lacked confidence. They didn't expect to win—and they often played that way. For Tim, this attitude was unacceptable. "I did my best, through my words and my example, to challenge my teammates to reach for something much more for themselves and for the team," Tim remembered.

With Tim at quarterback, the Nease High Panthers quickly changed course. They started winning games. And although they lost just as many as they won that year, some of the losses were close-fought games against powerhouse teams. For example, the Panthers went neck and neck with Palatka High, the top-ranked team in Florida, before losing in triple overtime. The Panthers realized that if they could play that way against Palatka, they could hold their own against anyone.

Turning Points

In the summer of 2004, between his sophomore and junior year, Tim traveled to the Philippines, the nation of his birth. He had not been there since the age of three.

In the Philippines, the BTEA ran an orphanage for about forty-five youngsters. Tim played with the kids there and spoke to them about God and the Bible. "I like just being able to minister to . . . the kids at the orphanage," he said, "because they don't have anything, and just to hug them and put an arm around them and talk to them makes a huge impact on their lives, and they're always going to remember that." In addition to ministering to the orphans, Tim traveled around the Philippines and preached to large groups of students.

Later in the summer, when Tim returned to Florida, he joined his teammates for off-season workouts and touch football tournaments against other high school teams from Florida and surrounding states.

Tim noted that his teammates played with more energy and confidence that summer.

That confidence immediately showed up at the start of the 2004 regular season. Nease won game after game. Midway through the season, the Panthers faced powerful St. Augustine. This team would not go down so easily. Nease led for most of the game, until St. Augustine took a 33–30 lead with only twenty seconds left to play. As the clock ticked down, Tim heaved a 70-yard Hail Mary pass (a long pass thrown in desperation) toward the end zone. No one caught it. Time was up. Nease had suffered its first defeat that year.

Tim and the Panthers took the loss in stride and continued their winning ways. With a 10–1 record for the regular season, they moved on to the Division 4A Florida high school playoffs. In the first playoff round, against Citrus High School, Nease won by the astronomical score of 76–6. But the next round brought Nease back to face St. Augustine, and once again, St. Augustine pulled out a victory.

The Panthers' season was over, but Nease High had become a force to be reckoned with in Florida high school football. And everyone recognized that Tim Tebow was the reason.

The Chosen One

High school football is more than just child's play. College coaches watch the high school season closely, looking for players who might be tough and talented enough to succeed at the college level. College football is big business. Championship college teams generate millions of dollars through ticket sales, merchandise sales, and television advertising. Many football fans are even more passionate about the college game than about the NFL. Alumni, or former students, are especially loyal fans of college teams. To keep the college football juggernaut moving, colleges need top-level players. So they send scouts to high school games to scour the field for young talent.

When Tim Tebow started playing for Nease High, college scouts noticed him right away. They began to send him recruiting letters. The

IN F◯CUS

Going for Broke

Even at the high school level, football players are used to playing in pain. Despite aches and bruises, pains and sprains, they keep playing to win. But during his sophomore year, in 2003, Tim Tebow took playing in pain to a whole new level.

In a game against Menendez High, a defensive lineman slammed into Tim as he released the football. Tim's leg buckled, and he limped off the field. It was just the first quarter, and the Panthers were down by 17 points. They could not afford to have their star quarterback sit out the rest of the game. So Coach Howard told Tim to get tough and sent him back on the field, bad leg and all. The Panthers clawed their way back. Late in the game, Tim scored on a 20-yard running play, tying the contest at 24–24. Menendez finished off the game with a winning field goal, and Tim hobbled off the field once again.

The team trainers knew Tim was hurt and rushed him to the hospital for X-rays. As it turned out, Tim had played most of the game—and even run the ball for a touchdown—on a broken leg.

first few were just form letters—generated by computer. But Tim was thrilled to receive them. He imagined himself playing for a championship college team. He also pictured himself playing in the NFL, on *Monday Night Football*, before a nationwide TV audience.

By the end of his junior year, recruiting letters were pouring in from all over the country. No longer computer-generated form letters, they were now personal, handwritten notes and cards from famous college coaches. The coaches offered Tim full scholarships—all tuition paid for four years of school—and promised to make him a starting quarterback. They invited Tim to visit them on campus to see their football facilities up close.

According to the rules of the National Collegiate Athletic Association (NCAA), Tim could make only five official visits to colleges to check out football programs. On official visits, the college foots the bill for the trip. But Tim could make as many unofficial, self-paid visits to colleges as he wanted. So along with his parents, he unofficially visited the University of Alabama, the University of Florida, Louisiana State University, the University of Miami, Ohio State University, the University of Michigan, the University of Southern California (USC), the University of Notre Dame, Boston College, and several other schools. For his official visits, Tim returned to Louisiana State, Alabama, Florida, USC, and Michigan.

By then the media had jumped on Tim's story. Journalists began to contact the Tebows. They wanted to write articles about Tim, the humble homeschooler who stood 6 foot 3 (1.9 m), weighed 225 pounds (102 kg), and could bench-press 315 pounds (143 kg) in the weight room.

Jacksonville-area filmmaker Ken Murrah wanted to make a movie about Tim's senior season at Nease. At first, Bob and Pam were hesitant to let the media intrude on their son's life. But they liked Murrah. They believed he would document Tim's talent in a positive way. Murrah also convinced the sports channel ESPN that Tim's story was worth telling. ESPN agreed to back the project.

Tim was flattered by the attention but also a little embarrassed. The film's title was *Tim*

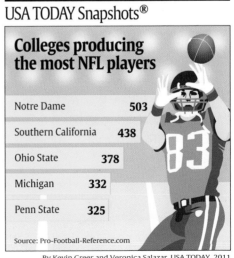

USA TODAY Snapshots®

Colleges producing the most NFL players

Notre Dame	503
Southern California	438
Ohio State	378
Michigan	332
Penn State	325

Source: Pro-Football-Reference.com

By Kevin Greer and Veronica Salazar, USA TODAY, 2011

Tebow: The Chosen One. This was a reference to all the colleges that wanted Tim to play for them. He was chosen in the sense of being highly sought after. Tim didn't like to boast and brag. He noted that the Bible teaches people to be humble. He didn't like to think of himself as "the chosen one"—no matter how many other people said he was special.

As Murrah was gearing up to make his documentary, Tim applied to attend the Elite 11 quarterback camp, sponsored by video game maker EA Sports. The four-day camp, held near Los Angeles, California, gives one-on-one coaching to eleven of the best high school quarterbacks in the nation. To make the Elite 11, Tim first attended a regional camp, where coaches evaluated his passing skills. Across the country, more than one thousand other high school players attended regional camps too. Coaches identified

One of the elite: Along with other talented young quarterbacks, Tim *(front, far right)* took part in the EA Elite 11 quarterback camp in California in 2005.

Tim as a standout at his regional camp, which put him in contention for the final cut—the Elite 11. Camp organizers then interviewed Tim and the other finalists by telephone and evaluated films of their high school games. The organizers recognized Tim's talent and chose him for the 2005 Elite 11. After attending Elite 11 camp, Tim returned to the Philippines to preach and to work at the BTEA orphanage.

Showtime

Every year ESPN broadcasts the High School Football Showcase—a series of nationally televised high school games featuring top-ranked teams from across the United States. Nease was scheduled to open its 2005 season with a Showcase game against Hoover High School from Hoover, Alabama, the number three team in the nation. The Panthers weren't nearly as strong as Hoover. They were ranked sixty-sixth in the nation. But ESPN wanted to showcase Nease anyway because of Tim's growing fame. The Panthers traveled to Alabama for the game. They hoped to upset their heavily favored opponents. For much of the game, the score stayed close. It was tied at 29–29 in the third quarter. But in the fourth quarter, Hoover pulled away with three unanswered touchdowns. The final score was Hoover 50, Nease 29. Tim hung his head and wept after the game.

Back in Florida, against their normal Jacksonville-area rivals, the Panthers got back to winning, putting up big numbers on the scoreboard for four games in a row. Then they came to that familiar bump in the road—St. Augustine, a team that had beaten Nease thirteen times straight. Some special visitors stood on the sidelines to see how Tim would perform in this big game. Mike Shula, the head coach at the University of Alabama, had been aggressively trying to recruit Tim for his team. He came to watch the game, as did several assistant coaches from the University of Florida. Tim wanted the win desperately, but again, St. Augustine came out on top. Again, Tim cried openly after the loss.

"He wants to win. He wants to play. I mean, he wants to complete every pass. Every game's the Super Bowl [for Tim]. Every down is the key down in the game. He's the ultimate competitor."

—Nease High football coach Craig Howard, 2005

The Panthers hit no more roadblocks after that. They powered through the rest of the regular season with no losses and again reached the state 4A playoffs. Tim had sprained his ankle in a regular-season game, so Coach Howard played him sparingly for the first playoff game. The Panthers won regardless. In the second playoff round, Tim again mostly sat on the sidelines, but he came in to help the Panthers beat New Smyrna Beach High School late in the game.

Showing speed: Tim showed off his sprinting skills after escaping an Armwood defender in Nease's win in the Florida state championship game.

Tim was back at full strength for the third round of the play-offs. During that game, Coach Urban Meyer of the University of Florida watched Tim and the Panthers beat Eastside High School. Like Mike Shula, Coach Meyer hoped Tim would choose to play college football for his school.

The victory over Eastside put Nease in the state finals, where they

Mobbed: Fans and media mobbed Tim after the state championship.

faced off against Armwood High. Armwood had won the state championships the previous two years. It was a hard-fought game, but the Panthers held on for a 44–37 win and the championship trophy.

Big Decision

Not only had Tim taken his team to a championship, he had set numerous Florida high school football records along the way. He racked up huge numbers for total offense (12,979), career passing yards (9,810), touchdowns (158), and completed passes (631). He was named Mr. Florida Football and played on the Florida All-State team.

And he wasn't just a football phenom. Playing in right field, Tim had helped the Nease High baseball team reach the state championships and had played on Florida's All-State high school baseball team. Many Major League Baseball (MLB) general managers had called Nease's baseball coach, wanting to set up meetings and tryouts with Tim. Some people, including Tim's dad, thought Tim should consider playing professional baseball, a career that paid better and put him at less risk for injury than football.

But for Tim, there was no question that he wanted to play football, not baseball. The only question was: which college should he choose?

He had eighty scholarship offers from top football schools. But by December 2005, he had narrowed the field to just two: the University of Alabama and the University of Florida. Both had strong, nationally ranked football programs. Both had recruited Tim aggressively.

When he had visited the University of Alabama for a football game, thousands of fans had cheered, held up signs, and shouted, "We want Te-bow."

Meanwhile, the University of Florida, in nearby Gainesville, was familiar territory for Tim. Both his parents had gone to school there. His sister Katie had attended Florida. His brother Peter was enrolled there. The Tebow home was filled with Florida Gator souvenirs. Even their mailbox had a Florida Gator

Familiar ground: Urban Meyer *(pictured)* coached the University of Florida Gators. Several members of Tim's family had gone to school there, and Tim followed suit.

football helmet on top. Tim liked Florida head coach Urban Meyer. Tim also felt that the Florida offense would be a great fit for him.

Tim planned to announce his choice on national television on December 13, 2005, right after receiving the Florida Dairy Farmers High School Player of the Year Award. But with only thirty minutes until the broadcast, he still couldn't decide which school to choose. Finally, "I gulped and picked one," Tim said. He chose Florida.

Helping out: Tim and the Gators played in Ben Hill Griffin Stadium, also known as Florida Field or the Swamp.

Into the Swamp

Tim wanted to start college early, in January 2006, to get a jump on training and to help Coach Meyer recruit more players to join the Gators. He wanted to meet with high school players who still hadn't chosen a college and encourage them to join him at Florida. Since homeschoolers can set their own pace, Tim and his mom had done extra schoolwork in the prior few years. That work allowed him to complete high school one semester ahead of schedule.

Only a month after Tim announced that he would attend Florida, he moved to Gainesville and started his first class, public speaking. The assignments were easy for Tim, since he had a lot of experience speaking in front of groups. He'd preached to big crowds in the Philippines, talked to TV reporters, and acted in plays at church.

Tim also started working out with the Florida football team, then coming off a 9–3 season. The workouts in the Florida Gymnasium, nicknamed Alligator Alley, were intense. Mickey Mariotti, Florida's strength and conditioning coach, put the players through a series of grueling drills. They ran up the stadium steps. They did push-ups and pull-ups with heavy chains hung across their bodies. Tim quickly showed that he could hold his own against his older teammates. The big linebackers and tackles were particularly impressed.

Greetings: A sculpture of an alligator greets football fans at Ben Hill Griffin Stadium.

Freshman Quarterback Reads More Than Defenses

From the Pages of
USA TODAY

Since coming to [the University of] Florida as a freshman in January, quarterback Tim Tebow has been hitting the books. His main subject: reading Division I-A defenses.

The physically impressive (6-3 [1.9 m], 225-pound [102 kg]) Tebow had a great prep career at Nease High School in St. Augustine, Fla., but never set foot in a classroom. That's because he has always been home-schooled.

"I'm used to getting one-on-one teaching from my mom," he said last week before receiving an award as the nation's top high school quarterback from the National Quarterback Club. "She gave me a desire for learning. It really doesn't matter how strong your arm is or how fast your feet are, because the most important thing is how you can read defenses."

Tebow hasn't been a backup quarterback since his freshman year of high school. He didn't sit on the bench, however, because he was a two-way starter as a tight end and linebacker.

He transferred to Nease his sophomore year and quickly erased several state records. In his 11–2 junior season, he threw for a record 4,286 yards and 46 touchdowns and rushed for 1,266 yards and 24 TDs. He led Nease to a state title as a senior and finished his career with 9,810 passing yards, 3,169 rushing yards, 95 passing TDs and 63 rushing TDs.

This season he'll probably spend most of his time learning [Florida] head coach Urban Meyer's high-powered offense while preparing to eventually replace starter Chris Leak. His football future seems bright, but Tebow says his religious upbringing helps keep his athletic career in perspective.

"First and foremost, my parents taught us about faith and character," he says. "Sure, you have to know about things such as geography, but it's more important to know who you are and what your place is in God's world."

His father oversees a large Christian ministry in the Philippines with more than 40 pastors and a 49-child orphanage. Tebow has spent his summers preaching in Philippine schools and public squares. He's active in the Fellowship of Christian Athletes and Campus Crusade.

"I haven't run into any resistance at Florida," he says. "(Former Gators quarterback) Danny Wuerffel was very outspoken about his faith. He's a role model of mine."

Tebow got off to a Wuerffel-like start in the spring Orange and Blue Game, where he led the Orange to a 24–6 win, completing 15 of 22 passes for 197 yards and a 16-yard TD pass. "That was my first game in The Swamp," he says. "It was really very exciting."

Tebow says winning a Southeastern Conference championship is one of his lifelong goals. "It is my biggest aspiration," he says. "That's what I am looking to do."

–Sal Ruibal

Learning the ropes: In the summer of 2006, Tim spent time learning Coach Meyer's system before his first football season at the University of Florida.

Number 15

Coming onto the field for his first college game, against Southern Mississippi, was a thrill for Tim. He wore number 15 on his jersey. The fans screamed and cheered as Tim and the other Gators ran through the stadium tunnel. They emerged onto Florida Field, nicknamed the Swamp.

Tim wasn't Florida's starting quarterback. The starter was Chris Leak—a senior. Tim was the number two man,

Waiting his turn: As a freshman, Tim posed with senior Chris Leak *(left)*, who was the Gators' starting quarterback.

but that role suited him just fine. "For me, more important than winning the [starting] quarterback job was earning some playing time, being part of the team, building the trust of the coaches and my teammates, and being able to contribute," he said.

For his first game as a college player, Tim was excited just to stand on the sidelines and feel the energy from the crowd. Early in the fourth quarter, with a 21–7 Florida lead, Coach Meyer put Tim in the game. The Gators needed 6 yards for a touchdown, and it was Tim's job to get the ball into the end zone. He was supposed to hand off to Kestahn Moore, but the snap came in low. So instead of handing off, Tim scooped up the ball, stiff-armed a defender, and dove into the end zone himself. Touchdown, Tebow!

Tim celebrated after making his first college touchdown. He ran around the field hugging his teammates. Florida went on to win the

Working together: Chris Leak embraced Tim after Tim made his first touchdown as a Gator.

game 34–7. After that first win, Coach Meyer played Tim for a least a few snaps every game—sometimes a lot more. Meyer often played Tim in short-yardage situations, where his strength and running ability helped him ram through the defensive line. Almost every time Tim played, he made an impact. In one big win, against Louisiana State, Tim scored each of the Gators' three touchdowns.

Big Man on Campus
Off the field, Tim kept busy. He went through long, hard workouts in Alligator Alley. He attended church on campus and joined several

associations for Christian students. He dated some female classmates, but none of the relationships got serious.

Tim hoped that someday, when his football career was over, he would use his people skills to earn a living. He especially wanted to work with kids, possibly at a nonprofit organization. To that end, he took courses in the university's family, youth, and community sciences program, along with communications classes. Because he was dyslexic, the university allowed him to take extra time to complete his examinations, but he usually didn't need it. In fact, Tim felt that his college classes were easy compared to his mom's rigorous homeschool lessons. He maintained a 3.76 grade point average.

Tim was something of a celebrity on campus. He had become famous across Florida the previous year, when he had led Nease to the state championship title. His fame continued as a freshman footballer, even though his playing time was limited. Student admirers—mainly females—often waited outside Tim's off-campus apartment. When he showed up on his way to or from school, they swarmed him, asking for an autograph. People regularly approached him in restaurants and other public places.

Tim used this fame to contribute to the community. Religious

Off the field: Tim visited with sick kids at Shands Hospital in Gainesville. His visits lifted the patients' spirits.

and other groups invited him to speak. He visited Gainesville's Shands Hospital every week and spoke to patients, encouraging them and often praying with them. Tim especially enjoyed visiting kids in the Shands pediatric ward. Tim also visited prisons and preached to the inmates there. He used a football metaphor to encourage the prisoners to turn their lives around. "I tell them that they might have had a bad first, second, or third quarter, but they can still have a great fourth quarter," he said.

The Boys of Old Florida

On November 11, Florida faced the University of South Carolina Gamecocks at the Swamp. By this time, the Gators had eight wins and only one loss (to Auburn University) for the season. If they beat South Carolina, they would clinch the Eastern Division of their football conference, the Southeastern Conference (SEC). The Eastern Division winner plays the Western Division winner for the SEC championship title.

The Gators were a bit shaky through much of the game. With the score tied 7–7 in the fourth quarter, coaches put Tim in to try to shift the momentum. The momentum shifted all right, but in the wrong direction. The Gamecocks moved the ball and took a 16–10 lead with eight minutes left on the clock. Tim and the Gators fought back for another touchdown.

"When it's all said and done, people aren't going to remember how many championships you won. They're going to remember what you were like off the field, how you treated people."

—Tim Tebow

July 27, 2006

Florida's Quarterback Frenzy; Senior Leak Remains the Starter, but Some Fans Can't Stop Talking about Heralded Freshman Tebow

<u>From the Pages of</u>
<u>USA TODAY</u>

The Florida Gators have one of the best quarterbacks in the country, a senior who has started every year and a player who has a shot at breaking the school record in passing yards. So why is Chris Leak seemingly the most unappreciated quarterback in the nation?

"Here's the bottom line," Florida coach Urban Meyer says. "If you're playing quarterback at Florida or playing quarterback at any school with tradition, you need to win a championship."

Which is something Leak hasn't done. But he did go 9–3 last year, beating Tennessee, Georgia and Florida State and leading the Gators to a victory against Iowa in the Outback Bowl.

Still, the Gators, who kick off fall practice in a little more than a week, should begin the season ranked in the top 10. So why are some Florida fans still debating who the starting quarterback should be? Meet freshman Tim Tebow.

Last December, ESPN aired a documentary entitled *Tim Tebow—The Chosen One* that chronicled his final season at Nease High School in St. Augustine, Fla. When the top prep quarterback selected the Gators over Alabama, the announcement was shown live on ESPNews and on local television and radio stations in Florida. When he arrived on campus in January, a semester early, the fervor intensified.

Not only is Tebow, 18, talented, he has a compelling personal story given his experiences traveling to the Philippines with his father on Christian mission trips. The Florida sports media relations office handles the numerous speaking requests Tebow receives. Not just from reporters, but from church and community groups across the South.

Famous freshman: Tebow answers questions from a group of reporters during the annual University of Florida Media Day in August 2006.

His first week on campus, Florida received 25 requests from different groups. Because he is comfortable speaking in front of large audiences—Tebow once spoke to a crowd of more than 10,000 at a summer mission trip—he gladly accepts those he can do, especially the ones involving children. Now the sports media office receives from five to 10 calls a week from groups looking to book Tebow for a speaking engagement.

During preseason practice and throughout the early part of the season, whenever 6-foot [1.8 m], 207-pound [94 kg] Leak has an off day or Tebow does well, Meyer will be asked about his quarterback controversy and he will repeat: "Chris Leak is our quarterback." But 6-3 [1.9], 225-pound [102 kg] Tebow, the No. 2, will play.

Tebow understands the pecking order. "It's a privilege to play behind him this season," he says of Leak.

—Kelly Whiteside

With his team up 17–16, Tim watched from the sidelines as the Gamecocks moved the ball downfield once again, landing in field goal range with a few seconds left in the game. When South Carolina lined up for the field goal, Tim couldn't bear to watch. He closed his eyes, held hands with some teammates, and prayed that the ball wouldn't make it through the uprights. It didn't. Gator Jarvis Moss blocked the kick, and Florida clinched the Eastern Division.

A few weeks later, on December 2, 2006, the 11–1 Florida Gators took on the 12–2 University of Arkansas Razorbacks for the SEC championship title. In the stands, Florida fans snapped their arms together like giant alligator jaws, a gesture called the Gator Chomp. They sang one of the school's fight songs, "We Are the Boys from Old Florida." On the field, the Gators dominated. Tim contributed one touchdown, helping the team to a 38–28 victory.

Winning ways: Gators hoist the trophy after winning the SEC championship game against the Arkansas Razorbacks in 2006.

On to Big Things

The Florida Gators were the SEC champions—a cause for great celebration in the locker room, on campus, and all across Florida. But there was more. At the end of the season, top college teams play in bowl games such as the Cotton Bowl and the Sugar Bowl. As the SEC champs, the Gators were certainly headed to a bowl game. But the day after the victory over Arkansas, the Gators got some fantastic news. They were headed to the biggest bowl game of all: the Bowl Championship Series (BCS) National Championship Game.

The BSC National Championship Game is like the Super Bowl of college football. The game is played between the two top-ranked college teams in the nation. It determines the one and only national champion of college football.

To figure out which teams are the top two, the BCS uses a complicated ranking system. It involves teams' win-loss records, conference standings, voting by coaches, and other factors. On the same day that Florida had beaten Arkansas for the SEC title, the University of California–Los Angeles had beaten the favored University of Southern California. USC's unexpected loss had shaken up the BCS rankings—and shot Florida to the number two spot. That meant Florida would play number one Ohio State for the title of national champion. (Beginning in 2014, the NCAA will use a four-team playoff system to determine the national champion.)

The BCS National Championship Game was Chris Leak's time to shine. At the game, played in Glendale, Arizona, on January 8, 2007, Leak completed 25 of 36 passes for 213 yards. The much-heralded Ohio State defense couldn't keep the Gators from scoring.

As the game unfolded, Tim waited patiently on the sidelines, ready to take over for Leak when called. Playing only a handful of snaps, Tim threw for one touchdown and ran for another. When the game ended with a 41–14 Florida victory, Chris Leak's college football career had officially come to a close—and Tim's time had finally come.

Tebow's turn: Tebow became the Gators' starting quarterback in his sophomore year at Florida. Here he greets fans after a win in 2007.

Big Yardage

When the college football season began in September 2007, all eyes were on Tim Tebow. Chris Leak had graduated, and Tebow had moved up to the number one spot as the Gators' starting quarterback. Could he live up to all the hype? Could he lead his team to another national championship?

No one had higher expectations than Tebow himself. "That moment of coming to the Swamp as the starting quarterback was something I'd looked forward to all off-season—not to mention my whole life," he said.

Florida's first opponent was Western Kentucky University—not a strong team. The Gators beat WKU easily and resoundingly, 49–3. Next up was Troy University, a good team but ultimately no match for the defending national champions. The Gators came away with a 59–31 victory.

Numbers Game

Few were surprised when Tebow and his teammates beat lesser opponents such as Troy. But how would they fare the following week against SEC rival Tennessee? That game would be the Gators' first chance to prove they were really a championship team.

The Gators proved it with a 59–20 blowout. "I think this makes us a front-runner for one of the top teams in the country," Florida receiver David Nelson said after the Tennessee game. "This is a statement that we're the defending national champions and we're not going to let anyone take it from us easily."

Most of all, the game showcased Tim Tebow's enormous talent. He completed 14 of 19 passes for 299 yards against Tennessee. He threw two touchdowns and ran for two others. Against the University of Mississippi the following week, he put up more big numbers. He threw for more

Showing off: Throughout the 2007 season, Tebow showed fans his football skills and his leadership in every game.

No stopping: Tebow used his body strength to escape defenders for a first down during a game at Ben Hill Griffin Stadium.

than 250 yards and rushed for 168. The combined total was a team record for a quarterback. Florida won that game 30–24.

Then the Gators stumbled. They lost to Auburn, 20–17, and then to Louisiana State, 28–24. These losses showed a chink in Florida's armor. The football pundits said that LSU, not Florida, looked like the championship team that year. But the pundits still couldn't stop talking about Tebow. Despite the losses, his numbers remained impressively high.

Crunch Time

Every year at the end of the college football season, sports journalists vote on the Heisman Trophy winner. Winning the Heisman is the highest individual honor in college football. The list of previous winners includes many players who went on to NFL superstardom. Only midway through the 2007 season, many sportswriters were already talking about Tim Tebow as a potential Heisman finalist.

Many quarterbacks rely on only the passing game. Tebow often ran with the ball, barreling right over defenders with his big body to make the first down or the touchdown.

His ability to both throw and run effectively set him apart from most other quarterbacks in the college game. But those running plays also put Tebow at risk for injury. In a game against the University of Kentucky, he took a big hit to the right shoulder. By the end of the game, he couldn't even lift his arm. (Since Tebow is left-handed, the injury didn't keep him from throwing the football.) That injury nagged him for the rest of the season. A few weeks later, against Florida State University, Tebow plowed up the middle from the 5-yard line for a touchdown. As he pushed at a defender's face mask with his right hand, another defender smacked into the hand with his helmet. Tebow felt something crack. He finished the game with a broken hand.

All Eyes on Tebow

By the end of the season, it was clear that Tebow was Heisman material. He had carried the ball 194 times, tallying 838 rushing yards and 22 rushing touchdowns. In the air, his numbers were just as spectacular. He had passed for 3,132 yards and 29 touchdowns and completed 68.5 percent of his throws. No other college quarterback had ever scored more than 20 rushing touchdowns and 20 passing touchdowns in one season.

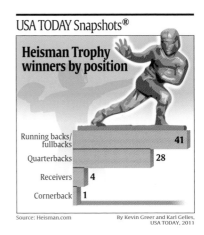

USA TODAY Snapshots®

Heisman Trophy winners by position

Running backs/fullbacks	41
Quarterbacks	28
Receivers	4
Cornerback	1

Source: Heisman.com

By Kevin Greer and Karl Gelles, USA TODAY, 2011

IN F⬤CUS

A Little Bit Country

Tim Tebow loves country music. Some of his favorite artists are Brad Paisley and Kenny Chesney *(right)*. Tebow's favorite song is "Where I'm From" by Jason Michael Carroll, a song that celebrates small-town life.

Once in early 2007, Tebow and some teammates went to see a Kenny Chesney show in Gainesville. The famous singer ended up inviting Tebow and his buddies onstage. They sang along with Chesney on his hit song "She Thinks My Tractor's Sexy," and Chesney put on a Gator football helmet.

The Gators as a whole hadn't fared as well. They had ended the season with three losses. They would not be playing for the SEC or the BCS title. But the team's less-than-championship season did not dampen the enthusiasm for their young quarterback. The honors came rolling in. Tebow won the 2007 Davey O'Brien Award as the best college quarterback in the country, the Maxwell Award as the nation's best college football player, the Sullivan Award as the nation's best amateur athlete, and several other awards.

On December 5, the Heisman Trophy Trust announced the finalists for the 2007 Heisman Trophy: running back Darren McFadden from the University of Arkansas, a junior; University of Missouri quarterback Chase Daniel, also a junior; Colt Brennan, a senior quarterback from the University of Hawaii; and sophomore quarterback Tim Tebow.

Tebow had played in big games and been on TV many times. But nothing could compare to the Heisman Trophy award ceremony, held at the Nokia Theatre in New York City on December 8. The sports media was out in full force. Twenty-seven former Heisman Trophy winners were in attendance. Florida coaches Urban Meyer and Mickey Mariotti had flown in for the ceremony. Craig Howard, Tebow's coach from Nease High, was there too. The whole Tebow family had come to New York. Even Tim's sister Christy and her husband, who were working as missionaries (religious teachers) in Bangladesh, a nation in southern Asia, flew in at the last minute. Tebow had never been to New York City before. He was swept up in the excitement.

Onstage at the Nokia, Brian D. Obergfell of the Heisman Trophy Trust stood next to the 25-pound (11 kg) bronze Heisman Memorial Trophy. Previous Heisman winners lined the back of the stage. Tim and the other finalists sat in the front row of the auditorium, waiting for Obergfell to name the Heisman winner.

"One of you tonight will join the elite Heisman fraternity," Obergfell said. "These gentlemen standing behind me are ready to welcome you in." A few moments later, Obergfell named the winner: Tim Tebow. Tebow beamed. He stood and hugged the other finalists and then hugged his parents and Coach Meyer.

Later that day, Tebow attended the Heisman Trophy award dinner. Dressed in a tuxedo and bow tie, he gave a moving speech. He said, "I want to be known not as a great football player but as a great person. I want to put God first, my family first, academics, and then football." Tebow also honored the past Heisman winners in attendance. "I'm just thankful to have this opportunity to join this band of brothers," he said. Finally, he saluted the city of New York. "In the words of Frank Sinatra, if you can make it here, you can make it anywhere," he concluded. The audience clapped and cheered.

USA TODAY

Sports
SECTION C

SPORTS.USATODAY.COM

December 10, 2007

Grateful Tebow has Heisman, Florida QB focuses on bowl game

From the Pages of USA TODAY   Soon after Florida quarterback Tim Tebow became the first sophomore to win the Heisman Trophy in the award's 73-year history Saturday night, he left the Nokia Theatre in Times Square and walked one block to the Hard Rock Cafe for a news conference.

Behind him were coach Urban Meyer and wife Shelley, pulled by the entourage undertow.

"I got whooshed behind Tim Tebow," Meyer said. "As it was pushing us, I said, 'This is kind of neat.'"

Did anyone even notice Meyer? "No. I was behind Tim," he said.

Next year, every other outstanding college football player will enter the season behind Tim, who will be favored to become the second player after Ohio State's Archie Griffin in 1974 and 1975 to win two Heisman trophies.

That feat seems entirely possible, considering Tebow has somehow managed to exceed the outsized expectations that greeted his arrival in Gainesville. During his freshman year, he played a key role in the Gators' national championship run. As a starter this year, Tebow became the first major-college player to run for 20 touchdowns and throw 20 TD passes in the same season.

Amid questions about his passing ability, he completed 217 of 317 passes for 3,132 yards and 29 touchdowns (and only six interceptions) and rushed for 838 yards and 22 scores, tying a single-season record for a quarterback.

Though some thought it would be a close race, given there was no clear front-runner until late in the season, Tebow easily distanced himself from Arkansas running back Darren McFadden, the first player since 1949 to finish second in consecutive seasons.

"It's awesome that you're known forever as a Heisman Trophy winner," Tebow said. He received 1,957 points and 462 first-place votes to McFadden's 1,703 and 291, respectively. Hawaii quarterback Colt Brennan was third and Missouri quarterback Chase Daniel fourth.

Minutes after accepting the trophy, Tebow was asked about the possibility of winning a second Heisman or even a third. "I've already been asked that a bunch of times. I'm just going to get ready for Michigan this year," Tebow said, referring to Florida's opponent in the Capital One Bowl on January 1.

The Gators (9–3) should be even better next season given

Awards: Tebow holds the Heisman Trophy at a press conference in 2007. That same year, Tebow won the Maxwell Award, the Sullivan Award, and other honors.

the experience their young players gained this year. "We don't lose many," Meyer said. "We have some very good young players."

Given Tebow's humble nature and his grounded priorities (faith, family, academics, football, he listed in that order), Meyer said all the inevitable talk about winning two or three Heismans won't be a distraction.

True to form, Tebow's response was the same. "I just have to get ready for Michigan," he said.

—Kelly Whiteside

A big night: Tebow poses with ESPN host Chris Fowler after winning the 2007 Heisman Trophy.

Tim Tebow was just twenty years old. He had become the first sophomore ever to win the Heisman Trophy. "Tebow Reaches the Top, but He Can Still Climb" read a headline in the *New York Times*. Since Tebow was a sophomore, he had at least one more year of college ball ahead of him. (After his junior year, he could go to the pros if he wanted.) Some reporters said that Tebow could very likely win a second Heisman Trophy during his junior year.

In the short term, Florida was scheduled to play the University of Michigan in the Capital One Bowl on January 1, 2008. Beyond that, Tebow was focused on the following season. "I'll be motivated even more and work harder than ever before," he said. "We've got to go 12–0 next year."

At the Capital One Bowl, the Gators played a fired-up Michigan team. The Michigan coach, Lloyd Carr, would be retiring after the game, after thirteen years as head coach. The Wolverines were determined to win this last game for Carr. And they did, with a final score of 41–35. Tebow looked beyond that disappointing end to the season. He wanted a 12–0 season in 2008, and he was determined to make it happen.

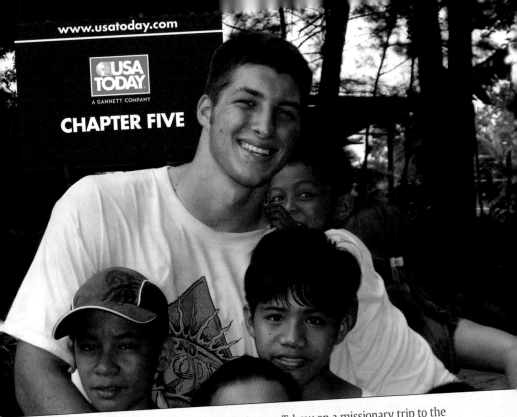

CHAPTER FIVE

Back in the Philippines: This photo pictures Tebow on a missionary trip to the Philippines in 2005. In the 2008 off-season, Tebow returned to the Philippines to continue his family's missionary work.

Out Front

Soon after the loss to Michigan in the Capital One Bowl, Tebow was back in class and back in Alligator Alley, working out harder than ever. Over the summer, he and his brothers made missionary trips to the Philippines, Thailand, and eastern Europe. Everywhere he went, he worked out. He ran on mountain roads and did exercises in airport terminals. He even did push-ups in the aisles of airplanes. He wanted to be ready for the 2008 season. He felt good about his team and their chances for an undefeated season—something Florida had never had before.

Focus

The Gators played their opener at home against Hawaii. Florida dominated, winning 56–10. But Tebow reinjured his right shoulder early in the game. It was a frustrating way to start the season.

The next opponent was Miami. Ahead of the game, Tebow hit on an interesting idea. Football players often wear black paint or black patches beneath their eyes. This "eye black" absorbs sunlight, cutting down on glare. It helps players see better on sunny days. Tebow was always looking for new ways to spread his religious messages, so he decided to write the number of a Bible verse on his eye patches. With a white marker, he wrote "PHIL" under his right eye and "4:13" under his left eye. This stood for Philippians 4:13, a verse that Tebow loved. It reads, "I can do all things through Christ who strengthens me."

Tebow never hesitated to bring his religious devotion to the football field. He always got down on one knee and prayed before and after games. The eye black gave Tebow another way to display his faith. He also hoped the writing beneath his eyes would make people ask questions. Then he could tell them about Philippians 4:13 and other Bible verses. In addition, the message helped Tebow get fired up before the game.

Florida easily handled Miami, with a 26–3 victory. The following week the Gators rolled over Tennessee with a 30–6 score. At 3–0, the Gators were off to a fine start.

Sending a message: Tebow used his eye black to encourage fans to read the Bible. He wrote the names and numbers of Bible verses, such as Romans 1:16, beneath his eyes.

"A Lot of Good Will Come Out of This"

The University of Mississippi, nicknamed Ole Miss, was the next team to face Florida that season. The Ole Miss Rebels came into the Swamp as underdogs. All the experts—coaches, commentators, and sports-writers—predicted a decisive Florida victory.

Early on, the game seemed to be playing out as expected. The Gators moved the ball well and had a 17–7 lead by halftime. But Tebow sensed that something was off. His team didn't seem sharp or confident. In the second quarter, receiver Aaron Hernandez fumbled the football, and in the third quarter, Tebow himself fumbled. He was sacked several times and missed open receivers. This sloppy play was uncharacteristic for Tebow and the Gators.

In the fourth quarter, Ole Miss tied the game at 24 and then went ahead 31–24 on a long touchdown pass. Tebow and the Gators needed

Not as expected: Tebow hugged teammate and top receiver Percy Harvin after a score in the game against Ole Miss. But the Gators lost in the final seconds of the game.

a touchdown. They got one, but the extra point was blocked. The score stood at 31–30 with just three and a half minutes left.

On their next possession, the Rebels had to punt the ball away. Tebow took over again and marched his team down to the Ole Miss 32. With 41 seconds left, the Gators faced a 4th and 1. They could have tried a field goal, but it would have been a risky 49-yard kick. Instead, Coach Meyer told Tebow to punch the ball over the line for the first down. This kind of running play—mowing through a row of defenders for short yardage—was Tebow's specialty. But it didn't work. Ole Miss stopped him for no gain. The seconds ticked down to zero. Ole Miss had beaten the mighty Florida Gators—and ruined their perfect season. The Gator fans and players were stunned.

Tebow was devastated. He sat in the locker room and cried. Finally, he pulled himself together and went to the postgame press conference. He felt a need to apologize to the Florida fans. Still fighting back tears, he gave a heartfelt speech:

> To the fans and everybody in Gator Nation, I'm sorry. I'm extremely sorry. We were hoping for an undefeated season. That was my goal, something Florida has never done here.
>
> I promise you one thing, a lot of good will come out of this. You will never see any player in the entire country play as hard as I will play the rest of the season. You will never see someone push the rest of the team as hard as I will push everybody the rest of the season.
>
> You will never see a team play harder than we will the rest of the season. God bless.

Tebow's impassioned speech made headlines. TV sports programs broadcast it over and over. CBS sportscaster Verne Lundquist called it one of the most memorable sports speeches of all time, comparable to Notre Dame coach Knute Rockne urging his team to "win one for the Gipper" (George Gipp, a teammate who had died) during the 1928

On a roll: Gators raise their helmets to celebrate a 49–10 win against Georgia in November 2008.

game against Army. Coach Meyer even had Tebow's speech engraved on a plaque and posted outside the football facility at Florida Field. The speech only added to Tebow's reputation as more than just a football player.

No Looking Back

Tebow's words inspired his teammates. The Gators roared back after the loss to Mississippi. They knocked off big victories against LSU (51–21), Kentucky (63–5), and Georgia (49–10). With a win over Vanderbilt University, the Gators clinched the SEC East. Then they rolled over Arkansas, South Carolina, The Citadel, and Florida State.

The SEC championship game featured the top two teams in the nation. Florida with its one loss was ranked number two. Alabama, which was undefeated, was ranked number one. The winning team would not only capture the SEC crown, but it would earn a trip to the BCS National Championship Game. Everything was on the line.

Going into the game, played in the Georgia Dome in Atlanta, Florida appeared to be at a disadvantage. Its top receiver, Percy Harvin, was out with a sprained ankle. Its leading runner, Chris Rainey, had a groin muscle injury. But Florida still had Tim Tebow, playing at full strength and determined to win.

After taking a one-touchdown lead into the locker room at half-time, the Gators found themselves down by three going into the fourth quarter. It was then that Tebow took charge. He led an eleven-play, 62-yard touchdown drive to put the Gators up 24–20. One more Florida touchdown would seal the deal, and Tebow was determined to get it. With just a few minutes left in the game, he hit receiver Louis Murphy for 33 yards, connected with Aaron Hernandez for another 15, and finished up with a 5-yard strike to Riley Cooper. Alabama could not recover. The final score was 31–20.

Champs again: Tebow's 5-yard pass to Riley Cooper (number 11) clinched the Gators' victory against Alabama in the SEC championship game in December 2008.

"[Tebow] has this aura [energy] about him, this feeling about him, this quiet confidence. He came into the huddle on that series [the last Florida drive]. He didn't say a word. He looked every single one of us in the eyes. He didn't say a word. We just all could tell by the look in his eye that he was going to lead us to victory."

—Gator David Nelson, after the SEC title game, December 6, 2008

After the game, Gator players hoisted the SEC trophy overhead as confetti rained down on top of them. The Gators were headed to another BCS championship game—and they had mainly Tim Tebow to thank for it. "I've seen some great players and I have a bunch of good players on this team," Coach Meyer said after the game. "But I've never had one like this [Tebow], and I've been around this game a long time."

Oklahoma!

Tebow was once again named a Heisman Trophy finalist. The others were quarterbacks Sam Bradford of the University of Oklahoma, Colt McCoy of the University of Texas at Austin, and Graham Harrell of Texas Tech. Shonn Greene, a running back from Iowa, was the only non-quarterback among the finalists. If Tebow won again, he would become only the second player in history to win the Heisman twice.

The voting was close, but in the end, Sam Bradford edged out McCoy, Tebow, Harrell, and Greene to win the big bronze statue. Tebow would soon get another shot to beat Bradford, however. The Gators were scheduled to play Bradford's Oklahoma Sooners in the BCS championship game on January 8, 2009. The winner would be named BCS National Champion.

December 12, 2008

Tebow prefers
championships to Heismans

From the Pages of
USA TODAY
After the 74th Heisman Trophy is awarded Saturday evening in Times Square, the winner will head to lower Manhattan for a news conference at the new Sports Museum of America. If that winner is Florida quarterback Tim Tebow, the museum might as well erect a new exhibit in his honor given the history involved.

Last year, Tebow became the first sophomore to win the award. If he beats out two other quarterbacks—Oklahoma's Sam Bradford and Texas' Colt McCoy—in what's expected to be an especially tight race, he would become just the second player to win the Heisman twice. Ohio State's Archie Griffin won in 1974 and '75.

"It would mean a lot," Tebow says. "It was great last year, something to look back on and cherish. It would be great again, but it doesn't compare to winning championships."

Though his 2008 statistics don't match his 32 passing touchdowns and 23 running TDs of last year—"Star Wars numbers," coach Urban Meyer says—Tebow has had a better season, according to his coaches. He led the Gators to a Southeastern Conference championship and now has a shot to win the national championship Jan. 8 against Oklahoma in Miami.

Tebow threw for 2,515 yards with 28 touchdowns and two interceptions, ranking No. 5 nationally in passing efficiency, and ran for 564 yards and 12 scores. He did this while facing six top-25 defenses and 10 top-50 defenses, based on current NCAA rankings. Without injured Percy Harvin, the team's most dangerous playmaker, he led the Gators to a fourth-quarter comeback in a 31–20 victory in the SEC title game against then-No. 1 Alabama.

During last year's trip to New York, Tebow didn't get to see much of the city, but he hopes to experience a bit more this time. "My family went out, but I never got to go with them shopping for fake Rolexes," he says.

That's OK. With one Heisman, and perhaps even two, Tebow will leave New York with the real thing.

—Kelly Whiteside

IN F🔍CUS

Google It

Before the Oklahoma game, Tebow changed the message on his eye black from Phil 4:13 to John 3:16. After the game, 94 million people searched for John 3:16 on Google to learn what the verse said. Tebow's goal of getting people interested in the Bible with his eye black had been fulfilled.

Tebow knew the Oklahoma game would be tough. Bradford and the Sooners had scored 702 points that season—the highest single-season total in college football. They had scored more than 60 points in each of their final five games of the season.

But when the teams took the field in Miami, the Gators showed who was tougher. With the game tied 7–7 at the half, Tebow turned on the jets. In the third quarter, he ran seven times for 52 yards, bringing the ball to the 2-yard line. From there, Percy Harvin took the ball into the end zone.

The Sooners scored to tie the game at 14, but the Gators moved ahead again with a field goal. With a little more than three minutes left, Tebow hit David Nelson with a jump pass—leaping into the air before throwing a strike from the 4-yard line. Oklahoma

USA TODAY Snapshots®

Most total yards in BCS Championship Game

Vince Young, Texas vs. Southern California, Rose, 2006 (267 pass, 200 rush)	467
Ken Dorsey, Miami (Fla.) vs. Nebraska, Rose, 2002 (362 pass)	362
Darron Thomas, Oregon vs. Auburn, BCS, 2011 (363 pass, -6 rush)	357
Tim Tebow, Florida vs. Oklahoma, Orange, 2009 (231 pass, 109 rush)	340
Cam Newton, Auburn vs. Oregon, BCS, 2011 (265 pass, 64 rush)	329

Source: BCSFootball.org

By Kevin Greer and Paul Trap, USA TODAY, 2012

couldn't answer. The final score was 24–14. The Florida Gators had their second national championship in three years.

"I'm just so proud of my teammates because they kept fighting for four quarters and that's how we were able to pull it out," Tebow said after the game. David Nelson added, "You can't script it better. It was the perfect ending to the perfect season."

Decision time: In 2009 Tebow could have chosen to enter the NFL draft, but he decided to finish his senior year at the University of Florida.

Hot Prospect

After his junior year, Tebow was eligible for the NFL professional draft. If he decided to go pro, he would move on to a big salary and a chance to test himself against the top players in football. Tebow definitely wanted to play in the NFL, but after talking with his parents, he decided to stay at Florida for his senior year. For one thing, he wanted to play one more season with Coach Meyer. He wanted the chance to win another BCS title. He figured the NFL could wait.

The 2009 season was filled with ups and downs. On the football field, the Gators racked up twelve straight wins for an undefeated regular season. At the same time, Tebow grappled with health problems. He injured his back at training camp in August. Three games into the season, he came down with the H1N1 virus, a severe flu. Despite the flu, he played the fourth game of the season, against Kentucky. During the third quarter of that game, Tebow took a big hit and everything went dark. An ambulance rushed him to the hospital. When he woke up in the hospital, the first words out of his mouth were, "Did we win?" In fact, the Gators had won the game, and Tebow had suffered a concussion, a jarring brain injury. He endured headaches on and off the following week but was well enough to play the next game against Louisiana State University.

Off the field, Tebow's senior year was busy and successful. He took part in a number of fund-raisers to help underprivileged and sick children. He completed classwork for his family, youth, and community sciences degree, finishing his college career with a 3.66 grade point average.

Tebow was once again nominated for the Heisman Trophy. He didn't win, but he won the William V. Campbell Trophy, given each year to the college football player with the best combination of academic

Another award: Tebow accepts the William V. Campbell Trophy from a representative of the National Football Foundation in December 2009.

achievement, community service, and athletic ability. This award is often called the Academic Heisman.

Everything on the Line

With their 12–0 record, the Gators were scheduled to again play Alabama in the SEC championship game. Most sports analysts expected Florida to win and to go on to the BCS National Championship Game. But the Gators faltered at game time. They fell behind in the second quarter and stayed behind. The final score was Alabama 31, Florida 13. This time, it was Alabama's turn to hoist the SEC trophy and take its spot in the BCS title game. Tebow cried on the bench as the game ended. "This is not how we wanted to finish our season in the SEC," he said. "It was frustrating. To say it wasn't would be a lie."

Instead of the BCS championship, Florida headed to the Sugar Bowl against the University of Cincinnati. Tebow had dreamed of playing for another national championship. The Sugar Bowl seemed like merely a consolation prize. He just couldn't get excited about the game. Still, he and the Gators had a big win over Cincinnati, 51–24. Tebow completed 31 of 35 passes for 482 yards—the biggest passing game of his college career.

A hard loss: Tebow's disappointment was obvious after his team lost to Alabama in the SEC championship game.

Where To?

Tim Tebow was ready for the big time—the National Football League. If college football is big business, then the NFL is megabusiness. Top professional football players sign multimillion-dollar contracts. They can earn millions more by appearing in commercials. Tebow needed an agent to handle the business end of his NFL career. He chose Jimmy Sexton of Memphis, Tennessee.

USA TODAY Snapshots®

Minimum salaries in four pro sports
(per week)

NHL (2010-11)	NBA (2010-11)	MLB (2011)	NFL (2010)
$9,615	**$9,108**	**$7,972**	**$6,258**

Source: World Features Syndicate   Note: For 52 weeks

By Kevin Greer and Veronica Salazar, USA TODAY, 2011

The NFL draft was scheduled for April 22 to April 24, 2010. Sexton wanted to make sure the NFL scouts got a good look at Tebow ahead of time. Sexton sent Tebow to the Senior Bowl in Mobile, Alabama. At this game, the best college seniors from the northern United States play the best college seniors from the South. No one takes the outcome of the game too seriously, but all the players want to shine on the field because NFL scouts attend in large numbers.

Tebow came down with strep throat a week before the game. He was sick with sores in his mouth and throat, couldn't eat for two days, and lost 16 pounds (7 kg). He played in the bowl game but played poorly (and his South team lost). The scouts were not impressed, but they also understood that Tebow had been ill.

But some scouts, coaches, and commentators were not impressed with Tebow at all—sick or well. The critics said he was far from the best quarterback in the NFL draft. Sam Bradford, Colt McCoy, and other prospects were much better, they said. Some said Tebow might not be picked until the third round of the NFL draft—maybe even later.

The critics picked apart Tebow's throwing style. They noted that his throws were often wobbly. They said he held onto the ball too long, giving defenders too much time to either sack him or block his throws. Tebow was accustomed to running with the football if he didn't spot an open receiver right away. This style of play wouldn't work in the NFL, where massive linemen will swarm and sack a hesitating quarterback in the blink of an eye. Even if Tebow did manage to move the ball on the ground, the experts said, his body would never hold up to repeated explosive hits by NFL linebackers.

A number of people argued that Tebow shouldn't try to play quarterback in the NFL at all. TV analyst and former Dallas Cowboys coach Jimmy Johnson was outspoken. He said, "I don't think Tebow can play in a pro-style offense, not quarterback. . . . Maybe he could be a tight end. . . . He's gotta play another position. He can't play quarterback."

Tebow had been hearing that same comment—that he was suited to be a running back, a tight end, or a halfback, not a quarterback—ever since Pop Warner football back in Jacksonville. The two national championships and the Heisman Trophy hadn't silenced the naysayers.

On the one hand, Tebow didn't worry too much about the criticism. As Jimmy Sexton reminded him, he didn't need to convince every NFL team of his talent—he just needed to convince one. "You only need one team to believe," Tebow said.

At the same time, Tebow didn't ignore the feedback. If NFL coaches thought he should make adjustments to his mechanics, he knew that he had better listen. He traveled to Nashville, Tennessee, to work out at a top facility, D1 Sports Training. Starting at seven in the morning, he did drills and weight lifting in the gym. In the afternoon, he worked with professional quarterback coaches. He focused on his passing game—his delivery, his footwork, and his accuracy. He threw thousands of passes. His goal was to speed up his release.

Tebow told reporters, "I want to be a quarterback in the NFL. That's been my dream since I was six years old. So I'm going to do what it

Convincing: Tebow showed off his superior running skills in early 2010. But football analysts were divided on whether he was ready to play in the NFL.

takes to do that. . . . You know, in high school they said I couldn't be a quarterback, and we've come a long way since then."

D-Day
On March 17, Tebow displayed his improved mechanics at the University of Florida's Pro Day, a workout in front of pro scouts. (Each big football school holds its own pro day before the NFL draft.) Some analysts were still skeptical about Tebow, but Josh McDaniels, the head coach of the Denver Broncos, saw greatness in the young player. McDaniels thought that with time and coaching, Tebow could develop into a star NFL quarterback.

The buzz around the NFL was that Denver wanted to draft Tebow in the first round but that the Minnesota Vikings and the Jacksonville Jaguars were also interested. But the NFL draft is unpredictable. As

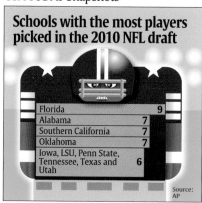

USA TODAY Snapshots®

Schools with the most players picked in the 2010 NFL draft

Florida	9
Alabama	7
Southern California	7
Oklahoma	7
Iowa, LSU, Penn State, Tennessee, Texas and Utah	6

Source: AP

By Matt Young and Alejandro Gonzalez, USA TODAY, 2010

the process unfolds, teams trade picks and change their preferences at the last minute, jockeying to get the guys they want to fill the positions they need. Sometimes, teams trade away picks from the following year to get a better pick in the current year—and vice versa. Teams also consider their budgets. Quarterbacks usually earn a lot more money than players at other positions.

Since the draft picture can change in an instant, no one knew exactly where Tebow would go until the pick was made. He hoped to be

Draft day: The stage was set at Radio City Music Hall in New York for the seventy-fifth NFL Draft in April 2010. Tebow chose to watch the event on TV from home.

Round and Round

The NFL is made up of thirty-two teams. Every year, teams draft the best players coming out of college. In theory, the team with the worst win-loss record gets the top pick, followed by the team with the second-worst record and on down the line. But in practice, the order of picking can be unpredictable, because teams often trade away their picks to get the combination of players they want at the salaries they can afford. After the first round of picks, teams go through six more rounds of picking.

Altogether, NFL teams selected 255 players in the 2010 draft. Oklahoma quarterback Sam Bradford, who won the Heisman the year after Tebow did, was the first player selected. He went to the St. Louis Rams. Denver picked Tebow with the twenty-fifth pick of the draft, in the first round. Quarterback Colt McCoy, the second-place winner in the Heisman voting in 2008, didn't get picked until the third round. The Cleveland Browns took McCoy with the eighty-fifth pick.

USA TODAY Snapshots®

Conferences with the most players picked in the 2010 NFL draft

Conference	Players
Southeastern	49
Big Ten	34
Atlantic Coast	31
Big 12	30
Pacific-10	28
Big East	18

Source: AP

By Matt Young and Keith Simmons, USA TODAY, 2010

chosen in the first round, but he knew he might go in round two, the following day, or even later.

The draft was held in New York City, at Radio City Music Hall. Many first-round prospects attended the event in person. But Tebow chose to watch the draft on TV with friends and family in Jacksonville. Several sports networks sent camera crews to Jacksonville to report on Tebow as he followed the draft.

April 23, 2010

Tebow steals prime-time show

<u>From the Pages of</u>
<u>USA TODAY</u>

A wild first round to christen the NFL's first three-day draft Thursday night included seven trades, a record-setting three Oklahoma Sooners in the top four picks, five defensive tackles . . . and one Tim Tebow.

The Denver Broncos' selection of Tebow—the Florida quarterback with two national titles and a Heisman Trophy on his resume but knocked by draft analysts for weeks—marked the biggest surprise at Radio City Music Hall in the league's 75th draft. Picked 25th, Tebow didn't attend the first prime-time NFL draft, which began with the St. Louis Rams taking quarterback Sam Bradford. But he was there in spirit.

Many projected Tebow as a second-round choice. "His intangibles were off the chart, and that appealed to the football people," said NFL Network's Mike Mayock, one of the few analysts who rated Tebow as a first-rounder. "He hit a low point at the Senior Bowl, but as the interview process went on, he showed how he changed his mechanics, and the football people got into him."

The draft continues with rounds 2 and 3 today, followed by rounds 4 to 7 Saturday. If the ensuing days follow the pattern of Round 1, expect more heavy bartering. Teams moved up and down the board with a flurry of trades. The San Diego Chargers jumped from 28th to the Miami Dolphins' 12th slot to draft Fresno State running back Ryan Mathews. The Philadelphia Eagles moved from 24th to the San Francisco 49ers' 13th position for Michigan defensive end Brandon Graham. And the Dallas Cowboys jumped three slots, to 24th, to draft Oklahoma State wide receiver Dez Bryant.

In the spotlight: The day after being drafted by the Denver Broncos, Tebow appeared at the team's headquarters in Colorado.

—Jarrett Bell

Wrong number: Tebow holds up a Denver jersey with his name on it, but he'd play as number 15, not number 10.

Back in New York, NFL commissioner Roger Goodell hosted the draft live. Down in Jacksonville, Tebow watched patiently as team after team picked player after player. The announcements went on for hours. Finally, sometime after ten thirty at night, Tebow's cell phone rang. Josh McDaniels was calling from Denver with the news Tebow had been waiting for. A few moments later, Goodell announced the pick on TV. Tebow was heading to the Denver Broncos.

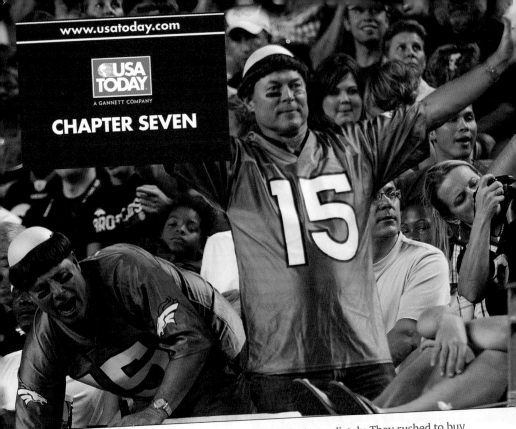

Instant connection: Denver fans embraced Tebow immediately. They rushed to buy Tebow jerseys from the NFL Shop.

Mile High Magic

Denver Bronco fans didn't care that some football experts still doubted Tebow—that some even said Denver had wasted its first-round pick on a questionable talent. As soon as the Broncos picked Tebow in the draft on April 22, Tebowmania took over Denver. As it does for all popular players, the NFL immediately produced replica Tebow football jerseys, in the Bronco colors orange and blue, with Tebow's name and number 15 on the back. In only one week of sales, the Tebow jersey was the top seller from NFLShop.com for the whole month of April.

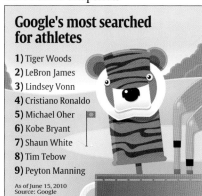

USA TODAY Snapshots®

Google's most searched for athletes

1) Tiger Woods
2) LeBron James
3) Lindsey Vonn
4) Cristiano Ronaldo
5) Michael Oher
6) Kobe Bryant
7) Shaun White
8) Tim Tebow
9) Peyton Manning

As of June 15, 2010
Source: Google

By George Artsitas and Paul Trap, USA TODAY, 2010

Denver's record the year before had been a lackluster 8–8. Fans needed a reason to believe that better days were ahead. That reason was Tim Tebow. Right after the draft, ESPN asked football fans to submit nicknames for Tebow to its website. The name that stuck was the Mile High Messiah. The "Mile High" part of the name referred to Denver, which sits 1 mile (1.6 kilometers) above sea level. *Messiah* means "leader" or "savior." Jesus is called the Messiah by Christians, and Tebow was being called the messiah of Denver football. The name was particularly fitting since Tebow is a devout Christian.

Down to Business

Tebow moved to Denver and rented a house. He lived with his brothers, Robby and Peter. Robby worked for Tim, helping him schedule appearances, media interviews, travel, and other non-football activities. As it happened, Peter was in divinity school in Denver, studying to be a minister like his father. The brothers got another housemate when Tebow adopted a dog from a breed called a Rhodesian ridgeback. Tebow named him Bronco.

Jimmy Sexton negotiated Tebow's contract with the Broncos. His salary for 2010 would be $1.3 million, with big raises in the following years, plus bonuses for superior play. Overall, the five-year deal added up to about $9.7 million. Tebow also signed high-paying contracts to endorse Jockey underwear and Nike athletic clothing. In the summer of 2010, Nike released a blue-and-orange Tim Tebow training shoe.

Tebow knows he has much work ahead

From the Pages of USA TODAY Tim Tebow smiles a lot—especially for an NFL rookie quarterback. The college legend retains an irrepressibly jaunty outlook, even in the face of squinty cynics who forecast a dim pro future for the Denver Bronco. "I love it," Tebow says, "when someone tells me I cannot do something."

The Tim Tebow Era commenced Sunday in Cincinnati. The 6-3 [1.9 m], 245-pound [111 kg] left-hander showed flashes of what Broncos coach Josh McDaniels, 34, saw in him in college: arm strength, maneuverability, toughness.

Several throws were impressive; a couple of others could have been intercepted. But it was an old mechanical flaw—slack in his delivery—that reared its ugly mane for the Bronco with the buzz cut. Tebow victimized himself on a safety blitz with a loopy, elongated motion that resulted in what initially was called a sack and fumble (later ruled an incompletion after instant replay).

Tebow finished 8-for-13 for 105 yards. He bulled his way into the end zone for a 7-yard touchdown on the game's final play, a run analyst Brian Baldinger says wasn't smart "because you won't survive in the NFL trying to bowl over linebackers."

Listed as Denver's No. 3 signal-caller behind starter Kyle Orton and backup Brady Quinn, the rookie is not ready for prime-time exposure. Unlike recent rookie quarterbacks who started immediately and played well, including the Atlanta Falcons' Matt Ryan and the Baltimore Ravens' Joe Flacco, Tebow faces no such expectations from the Broncos. "You won't talk to many quarterbacks or reputable quarterback minds who feel that he is going to be successful anytime soon," says Trent Dilfer, the Super Bowl-winning ESPN analyst.

Dilfer says he was "absolutely shocked" when McDaniels snatched Tebow in the first round of April's draft. Tebow remains what McDaniels suspected he was when the second-year coach selected the football-playing missionary with the 25th overall pick—a work in progress.

Tebow has struggled with transferring what he comprehends in the meeting rooms to the practice field, where junkyard-dog defenses bite back. Observes Orton:

"He looks like all high-draft-pick rookies—good plays, bad plays. He certainly shows glimpses of, 'Hey, that's pretty good.'"

McDaniels thinks the scrambler's versatility makes him unpredictable and problematic for defenses. McDaniels would love to see Tebow, a double threat, master enough plays out of the Wildcat offense to justify making him Orton's backup.

The most-repeated predraft criticism of Tebow was his unrefined delivery. In college, Tebow's low-slung, slower release and imprecise footwork were not issues. With Tebow in the shotgun, the receivers were often superior athletes who effortlessly outplayed defenders.

In the NFL, quarterbacks operate in what Dilfer calls the "cluttered space"— where a quick, compact delivery is often

Unconventional form: Critics attacked Tim's throwing style. They said he held on to the ball too long.

the difference between a completion and a sack. McDaniels does not sound overly preoccupied, at least publicly, regarding his protégé's mechanics. "He may look different (than most NFL quarterbacks), but that doesn't matter," McDaniels says. The coach also likes Tebow's accuracy and ability to put a fine-artist's touch on the football. "He uses touch and zip. He has not disappointed us in that area," says McDaniels, who is most impressed with Tebow's game above the shoulder pads. Tebow's work ethic cannot be questioned, particularly when he has something to prove.

Tebow has a college pedigree that produced two national titles and a trough full of records. Tebow was rewarded when he signed a five-year contract last month guaranteeing him $9.79 million.

"Tebow-mania" has migrated from its Southern roots. The team's first practice in suburban Denver drew more than 3,000 people. Tebow regularly signs autographs for the orange crush [crowds of Bronco fans] that is held in check by multiple guards.

"He just kept signing and smiling, signing and smiling," says Linnea Schramm, a Florida grad. "He never got ruffled or was rude. He never looked bored. He just had that big smile."

—Jon Saraceno

Still learning: Tebow listens in as Broncos' coach Josh McDaniels talks to starting quarterback Kyle Orton during the 2010 season.

Tebow did not let all the big money distract him from his new job. He trained with the Broncos all spring and summer. The team already had two other quarterbacks, Kyle Orton and Brady Quinn. Both had several years of NFL experience under their belts. Tebow knew he'd be the bottom man on the totem pole. The coaches wanted to introduce him to NFL play slowly. They told him not to expect much playing time during his rookie season. Tebow was content to watch, listen, and learn. He had played only minimally during his first season at Florida. He knew this first pro season would be similar.

Bad News Broncos

The Broncos played their 2010 season opener against the Jacksonville Jaguars in Jacksonville, Tebow's hometown. The Jags usually had a hard time filling their stadium. But this game was a sellout. Local football fans came to cheer Tebow in his first pro game—even if he was playing for the opposing team. Many fans were dressed in Broncos jerseys with Tebow's name and number, 15.

But Tebow barely played in the game. He came in for only two downs, rushing for a 1-yard gain each time. The final score was Jacksonville 24, Denver 17.

It was a disappointing start to the season, and it soon became clear that the season might not get much better. The once-mighty Denver Broncos did not have a strong team. Starting quarterback Kyle Orton had played some decent seasons with the Chicago Bears, but he was no superstar. The number two QB, Brady Quinn, had had three ho-hum seasons with Cleveland. The rest of the team was filled with "undrafted rookies, unwanted free agents, aging veterans, and unproven youngsters," wrote Denver sportswriter Mike Klis.

And of course, Denver had Tim Tebow. But after the loss to Jacksonville, Tebow didn't play for the next five games. Meanwhile, the Broncos lost three more games and won two. Fans started to grumble. Why wasn't Coach McDaniels playing Tebow? Tebow finally went in against the New York Jets in mid-October. He rushed six times for 23 yards and scored his first NFL touchdown. But Denver still lost the game, 24–20.

Tebow sat out the next week, a loss to the Oakland Raiders, but played the following week against the San Francisco 49ers. His overall playing time was limited. The team kept losing, and fans were unhappy. Home games at Denver's Invesco Field were poorly attended. Fans even booed the players as they went into the locker room at halftime.

When asked why he didn't play Tebow more, Coach McDaniels insisted that Tebow was a long-term project for Denver. McDaniels was developing Tebow for the team's future, he said, not for 2010.

While McDaniels was focused on the future, the team's season was circling the drain. By early December, the Broncos were 3–9. Broncos

IN FOCUS

Flying Colors

Dressed in his new Bronco uniform, Tim Tebow looked a lot like he had as a Florida Gator. Both teams have blue and orange uniforms. Tebow's jersey number in college had been 15. He kept the same number as a Bronco.

His chance: Tebow got his chance to play at the end of the 2010 season. Here he escapes a sack during a game against the Houston Texans.

owner Pat Bowlen had had enough. He fired Coach McDaniels and re-placed him for the rest of the season with running backs coach Eric Studesville.

Better Late Than Never

The season was lost. Denver sat in last place in its division, the AFC West. Bronco fans were disgusted. But in mid-December, with only three games left in the season, fans got a glimmer of good news. Coach Studesville announced that Tim Tebow would finally start at quarterback.

If Tebow played well, he could at least restore a little dignity to the Broncos franchise. He could also show the coaches that he was starting quarterback material going into the next season. Tebow was determined to come through for the fans. In his first start, against the Oakland Raiders, he threw for one touchdown and ran for another. But Denver still lost the game, 39–23.

The next game, at home in Denver, the stadium was nearly full. Even though it didn't matter if the team won or lost, fans came out to watch Tebow start another game, this one against the Houston Texans. At first the situation looked grim. By halftime, the Broncos were down 17–0. But they clawed their way back. By the fourth quarter, the score was 23–17, with Houston still on top. Tebow led a final touchdown drive to seal a 24–23 victory. The fans in Invesco Stadium erupted with cheers. Sure, the season was lost. But Tim Tebow was a winner.

The Broncos lost the final game of the season, against the San Diego Chargers, but the fans still cheered as Tebow and his teammates walked off the field. Tim Tebow gave them reason to hope for brighter days ahead.

IN F⊙CUS

The Tim Tebow Foundation

In January 2010, Tebow launched the Tim Tebow Foundation. This charity carries out Tebow's goal of helping people around the world, both spiritually and physically. The foundation has four main programs:

* Through the W15H program, Tebow meets personally with children with life-threatening illnesses.
* The Cure International Partnership provides health care to physically disabled children in poor nations.
* The foundation builds Timmy's Playrooms in children's hospitals around the world.
* The foundation supports Uncle Dick's Orphanage in the Philippines. The orphanage was founded by Tim's father, Bob, and was named after Richard Fowler, a Tebow family friend and neighbor.

New management: Celebrated Denver quarterback John Elway *(left)* shakes the hand of Broncos owner Pat Bowlen, as Elway is introduced to the media as the team's new vice president of football operations.

Comeback Kid

Denver Broncos football underwent a big shakeup in the winter of 2011. Broncos owner Pat Bowlen hired the most famous man in the history of Denver football, former Super Bowl–winning Bronco quarterback John Elway, to be the Broncos' executive vice president of football operations. Elway hired John Fox to be the team's new head coach.

The change in management left Tim Tebow in a vulnerable position. Josh

McDaniels had handpicked Tebow one year earlier in the NFL draft. McDaniels had been committed to making him Denver's starter down the line. Elway and Fox had no such allegiance to Tebow. Like many other football bigwigs, they were skeptical of Tebow's skills. They were not sold on him as a starting quarterback. In fact, they wanted to stick with Kyle Orton heading into the 2011 season. Performing well in the preseason, Tebow did move ahead of Brady Quinn to take the number two spot behind Orton. But number two was not number one. Tebow was back on the bench.

Déjà Vu

The beginning of the 2011 season looked pretty much like the beginning of the 2010 season for the Denver Broncos. Kyle Orton played badly. Tim Tebow stood on the sidelines. Denver lost three games out of its first four. Fans at Sports Authority Field (the new name for Invesco Stadium) held up signs reading, "We Want Tebow." This year, however, the coaches didn't wait until game 15 to respond to a desperate situation.

Fan favorite: Broncos fans showed their support for Tebow—and their wish that new coach John Fox would put him in the game.

Against San Diego: Tebow got his chance in the second half of the game against the San Diego Chargers. The Broncos lost, but Tebow won the starting quarterback slot.

In game 5, against the San Diego Chargers, the Broncos found themselves down 23–10 at the half. Enough was enough. Coach Fox pulled the plug on Orton and sent in Tebow to play the second half. With Tebow at the helm, the Broncos started chewing away at the San Diego lead. By the fourth quarter, Denver trailed by just 5 points. Tebow hurled a Hail Mary on the final play, but it landed on the turf. Although the Chargers won the game 29–24, Tebow's gritty play had reenergized the team. After the game, Coach Fox made it official: Tim Tebow would be his new starting quarterback.

In the next game, against Miami on October 23, Tebow pulled out a spectacular come-from-behind victory, bringing his team back from 15–0 to win the game in overtime. This was also the game that ignited the Tebowing craze all over Denver and beyond. Finally, Denver football fans had something—someone—to cheer about.

"You've Been Tebowed"
The following week, against the Detroit Lions, Tebow and the Broncos played poorly. The Lions kicked Denver around the field in a 45–10 rout. But after that, Tebow orchestrated a string of resounding victories. On November 6, the Broncos beat the Oakland Raiders 38–24. Tebow rushed for 117 yards and passed for 124 yards in the game. The next week the Broncos outplayed the Kansas City Chiefs, winning

17–10. Four days later, in a special Thursday night game, Tebow and the Broncos came from behind to beat the New York Jets, 17–13. The Broncos record stood at 5–5 for the season.

The next week the Broncos again faced the San Diego Chargers. This time, down 13–10 in the fourth quarter, Denver tied the game with a 24-yard field goal. The game went to overtime, where Denver won it with another field goal.

The come-from-behind victory was starting to look like Tim Tebow's specialty. The fans cheered loudly for their comeback quarterback, but the critics were just as loud. If a quarterback specialized in come-from-behind victories, they pointed out, that meant he spent a lot of time being behind in the first place. A great quarterback needed to play well from start to finish, the pundits said, not just pull miracles out of his hat in the last minutes of a game.

As the pundits ran on at the mouth, Tebow kept pulling off miracles. In another comeback victory, the Broncos edged out the Minnesota Vikings, 35–32, in week 13. Then, after overcoming a 10–0 deficit in the fourth quarter, the Broncos beat the Bears in overtime.

By then the term *Tebow* had entered the Denver dictionary, with several different meanings. If someone got down

Tebow Time: When Tim worked his fourth-quarter miracles, fans called it Tebow Time.

USA TODAY Snapshots®

Most influential athletes

1 Lance Armstrong, cycling

2 LeBron James, basketball

3 Tim Tebow, football

4 Shaun White, extreme sports

5 Shaquille O'Neal, basketball

Source: Encino E-Poll Market Research via Forbes.com

By George Artsitas and Alejandro Gonzalez, USA TODAY, 2010

on one knee the way Tebow did before and after games (whether praying to God or just praying for a Denver victory), that person was Tebowing. If a team was beat late in the game, it had been Tebowed. If the game was on the line in the fourth quarter, it was Tebow Time. And of course, Tebowmania was the all-out devotion to Tebow and everything he stood for.

Show's Over

The Broncos were 8–5 after the win over Chicago. Tim Tebow had done more than reignite the passions of Denver football fans. He had also led his team steadily up the AFC West standings. If the Broncos continued to win, they could very well secure a spot in the NFL play-offs. As this possibility became clear, Tebow's critics quieted down.

In week 16, Denver faced the New England Patriots, Super Bowl champs in 2002, 2004, and 2005. With their superstar quarterback Tom Brady, the Patriots were too much for the Broncos to handle. New England won the game 41–23. A week later, the Broncos lost again, to the Buffalo Bills, by a score of 40–14. Tebow's play was sloppy in the Buffalo game. He played poorly again the following week—against quarterback Kyle Orton, who'd been released by Denver and signed by the Kansas City Chiefs. The Chiefs came away with a 7–3 victory.

Three back-to-back losses certainly took the air out of the Broncos' sails. But their 8–8 record put them at the top of the AFC West standings, in a three-way tie with Oakland and San Diego. To break the tie, the NFL analyzed how each of the three teams had fared head-to-head against one another. Then it looked at the three teams' records within the AFC West, as well as against common opponents. In this three-part

Tebowing: High school students copy Tebow's kneel-down pose during a tight basketball game.

analysis, Denver came out on top. The Broncos were division champs and were headed to the first round of the NFL playoffs. Denver hadn't had a playoff appearance since 2005.

"Pull the Trigger"

The Broncos certainly didn't boast or brag heading into the playoffs. After all, they were coming off a three-game losing streak. They had won the division with a mediocre 8–8 record. Making matters worse, Denver was matched up in round one against the powerhouse Pittsburgh Steelers, one of the most celebrated teams in professional football. Pittsburgh had won six Super Bowls—more than any other team in the NFL—with its most recent championship in 2009. In 2011 the Steelers had a strong 12–4 record and the top-ranked defense in the league. Few people gave the Broncos much of a chance against Pittsburgh, even though the Steelers' defense had lost a number of players to injury.

John Elway, Denver's VP of football operations, knew his team was discouraged. But he believed the Broncos could hold their own against Pittsburgh—especially if Tebow executed. "The key thing for [Tebow] is to go out . . . and pull the trigger," Elway told a *Denver Post* reporter. "When you get into these playoff situations, he's a good enough athlete, you know what, to pull the trigger."

Tebow had played in big games before, but his first NFL playoff was the biggest ever. Denver fans mobbed Sports Authority Field to see if the Mile High Messiah could indeed pull the trigger against Pittsburgh. Almost 80 percent of Denver-area households were tuned in on TV.

The first quarter was bleak. Tebow couldn't complete a pass. The Steelers didn't play much better, but they did manage to score two field goals to take a 6–0 lead. In the second quarter, Tebow stepped up his game. He threw for one touchdown and ran up the middle for another. Placekicker Matt Prater added two field goals. By halftime, Denver had taken a 20–6 lead.

A playoff win: Tebow thrilled Broncos' fans and stunned the nation by leading Denver to an unexpected win against the Pittsburgh Steelers in January 2012.

The Steelers came back strong in the second half. By the end of the game, as the clock ticked down, the score was tied 23–23. This one was going to overtime.

Quick Strike

It was over practically in a blink of an eye. On the first play in overtime, Tebow fired a 20-yard pass to wide receiver Demaryius Thomas. Thomas snagged the ball at midfield, stiff-armed a defender, and sprinted 60 yards into the end zone. In just eleven seconds, the game was over. Denver had knocked off Pittsburgh to advance to the next round of the playoffs.

Excited, Tebow took a victory lap around the stadium, slapped the hands of exultant fans, and then jumped into the stands himself. He landed in the arms of screaming fans. When the crowd finally let go of him, Tebow ran back into the end zone, got down on one knee, put his fist to his forehead, and thanked God.

Watching the overtime victory in the CBS television studio, the commentators at *NFL Today*—James Brown, Bill Cowher, Dan Marino, Shannon Sharpe, and Boomer Esiason—were flabbergasted. They could think of just one way to appropriately sign off their broadcast. The five big men put their fists to their foreheads and Tebowed.

Afterward: Tebow celebrated with fans after winning against the Pittsburgh Steelers.

January 10, 2012

It's Tebow Time

From the Pages of
USA TODAY
Tim Tebow is a one-man cultural blitz. The Denver Broncos quarterback—a fervid evangelical with more devotion than downfield passing skills—took 11 seconds to rip off the longest overtime touchdown pass in the shortest overtime in playoff history Sunday night, lofting his team into the second round of the NFL playoffs.

"Hyperbole is almost impossible," says Tom Krattenmaker, author of *Onward Christian Athletes*. "His piety and his outspoken evangelical commitment are interesting, but they wouldn't matter if not for the incredible drama and success he brings to the football field."

Now, Tebow talk has swept the nation. His against-all-odds heroics brought CBS a mind-blowing 25.9 overnight rating, the best for a wild card football game in almost 25 years. Sports websites staggered under an onslaught of hits. NFL.com reported views of videos in the hour after the game up 385% over Wild Card Sunday last year.

Tebow hit more than 1 million mentions on Twitter. Sunday night, the rate of tweets announcing the victory hit 9,420 per second. Both Tebow and his favorite Bible verse, John 3:16 (proclaiming Jesus' promise of salvation), were in the top three Google Trends throughout most of Monday. NFL sales of Tebow's No. 15 Broncos jersey are second only to those for Green Bay Packers QB Aaron Rodgers, who won the Super Bowl last year.

"When someone like Tebow emerges—charismatic, impressive and pure on and off the field—you feel proud," Krattenmaker says. "You just don't want to take it too far and get silly. God doesn't wax and wane like a football player's success."

Not everyone is thrilled. Recently, former Broncos quarterback Jake Plummer told a Phoenix radio show that Tebow should chill out the God talk and just go hug his teammates after a victory. "I don't hate him," Plummer said. "I just would rather not have to hear (about Jesus) every single time he takes a good snap or makes a good hand-off." Tebow, the son of a missionary and a homeschooling mom, replied to Plummer's criticism with more praise for Jesus.

Tebow was No. 11 on the annual USA TODAY/Gallup list of most admired men in the nation, topping the Dalai Lama. The votes were cast back when the Broncos were still on the playoff bubble. "Tebowing"—dropping to one knee in prayer anytime anyplace—is a national phenomenon.

Tebow's autobiography, audaciously written when he was a 23-year-old second-string QB most critics called a miscast running back, came out in June. *Through My Eyes* was the best-selling religion book of 2011 for publisher HarperOne.

If his success continues, he could become God's gift to marketing. His current corporate partners include Jockey, Nike and FRS Energy drinks. Jockey has launched a $1 million "Super" challenge, offering $1 million worth of Jockey products to 40,000 fans if Tebow leads the Broncos to a Super Bowl XLVI victory.

Mark DeMoss, head of [the DeMoss Group], an evangelical public relations firm, says Tebow managed to "capture the love and hate of most of America even though no one has actually heard him give a sermon. We just see him kneel and pray and put Scripture passages in the public eye."

There was certainly nothing predestined about Tebow's journey to the peak of the nation's consciousness. Amid public doubts from Broncos management that he could be the team's long-term answer at quarterback, Tebow took the starting job from Kyle Orton entering Week 7 as Denver foundered with a 1–4 record. He immediately led the team to an overtime victory over Miami. "Tebow Time" was born, and after a 45–10 walloping at the hands of the Detroit Lions, Denver won six in a row, including overtime thrillers against the San Diego Chargers and the Chicago Bears.

During the stretch, Tebow had one of the NFL's worst passer ratings among starters in the first three quarters of a game, and the league's third best in the fourth quarter and overtime. Against Chicago, he earned his sixth game-winning drive in the fourth quarter or overtime in his first 11 starts, a Super Bowl-era record for a quarterback.

Blowout losses to the New England Patriots and Buffalo Bills followed, and the Broncos fell 7–3 to division-rival Kansas City in a game that would have clinched the AFC West division and a playoff berth. But the Oakland Raiders dropped the ball that same Sunday, and Denver (8–8) became the 13th team since 1970 to make the postseason with an even or losing record.

Regardless of whether Tebow the football player triumphs, Tebow the evangelical has already won. Brad Pappas, 28, of Denver, a first-year season-ticket holder, longtime Tebow fan and a Christian but not a churchgoer, said Monday that he opened a Bible to check out John 3:16. "If that's where Tebow gets his inspiration, nothing wrong with trying that."

—Cathy Lynn Grossman

End of the Road

After dispensing with the Pittsburgh Steelers, the Broncos faced an even tougher opponent in the next round, the storied New England Patriots. This time, Tebow didn't pull off any last-minute heroics. Under the steady leadership of quarterback Tom Brady, New England scored early and often. Tebow floundered and fumbled. The final score was New England 45, Denver 10.

IN F⊙CUS

Best Seller

In early 2011, Tebow wrote his autobiography, *Through My Eyes*, with the help of professional writer Nathan Whitaker. In the book, Tebow tells his story from his birth in the Philippines through his first NFL season. Shortly after publication, the book hit the best-seller lists.

Through his eyes: Tebow signs copies of his best-selling autobiography, *Through My Eyes.*

At the press conference after the game, Tebow spoke positively about the up-and-down 2011–2012 season, his teammates, and his opponents. He said that he was going to continue to learn from his mistakes and become a better football player. He summed up his playing philosophy this way:

> Any time you're getting beaten like that [during the New England game], you just continue to fight. It doesn't change who you are, how you play, how you go out there—you should be the same at all times. That's what I wanted to show and it didn't matter if it was the first play or the last play or if we were down by 42, I was going to be the same player and I was going to still give everything I have because that's all I have to give. Every time I step on the field, I'm going to give my whole heart regardless of the score.

As always at the end of the season, Tebow knew where he was headed: back to the weight room and back to the practice field. What were his plans for the off-season? He was going to "just work and improve," he told reporters.

"I'm not just looking forward to the destination, but enjoying the journey and just living out my dream as well as trying to get better. It's definitely not Super Bowl or bust. I'm having fun every day. Whatever happens, I'll definitely count this season as a blessing."

—Tim Tebow, after the playoff victory over Pittsburgh, 2012

USA TODAY
A GANNETT COMPANY

EPILOGUE

Not easy: Tebow and Elway (*left*) had a prickly relationship while Tebow was in Denver.

When You're a Jet

The fans loved Tim Tebow. The press loved Tim Tebow. Tim Tebow filled stadiums, made headlines, and sent TV ratings soaring. Some people even said that Tebow should run for president. But at least one person wasn't so crazy about Tim Tebow at the end of the 2011 season. That person was John Elway, the top football executive for the Denver Broncos.

Sure, Tebow had orchestrated a series of amazing comebacks in 2011. But that didn't make him a great quarterback. Many analysts noted that his passes were still wobbly. His delivery was still slow. He had completed only 46.5 percent of his passes in 2011. He still made most of his best plays as a runner. In short, he was not the kind of quick-draw quarterback that an NFL team needed to win football games consistently.

Elway found it annoying to have rabid fans clamoring for Tebow even though his play was spotty. Elway didn't care about Tebowmania. He just wanted a consistent passing quarterback with a proven track record. He wanted to win games. So when superstar quarterback Peyton Manning announced that he would be leaving the Indianapolis Colts after fourteen seasons (including one Super Bowl victory and four MVP awards), Elway went into action. He signed Manning to a rich five-year contract.

Snapped up: Elway jumped at the chance to bring in veteran and outstanding quarterback Peyton Manning.

In New York: The result of Elway's decision was that Tebow was traded to the New York Jets. Here he greets the New York media for the first time as a Jet.

That left the question of what to do with Tim Tebow. Elway could just leave him on the Denver bench and let Tebowmania simmer and swirl around him. But Elway didn't want that distraction. He quickly made a deal to trade Tebow to the New York Jets for two draft picks. The whole transaction happened superfast. On March 19, 2012, Manning announced that he was joining the Broncos. By March 21, Tim Tebow was a New York Jet.

The Tebow trade gave sportswriters plenty to talk about. Would Tebow take the starting spot from Jets quarterback Mark Sanchez? How would Tebow fit in with the Jets' wildcat offense? How would country-and-western Tebow survive in rock-and-roll New York City? How would the pious Tebow get along with Jets coach Rex Ryan, famous for lacing his speech with curse words?

If Tebow was unhappy about the trade to the Jets, a team with an 8–8 record for 2011, he certainly didn't let on. If he was unhappy about playing backup to Sanchez, an often ineffectual quarterback, he sure didn't show it. At a press conference after the trade, Tebow was typically upbeat. He said he had no hard feelings about being traded. "I understand what they [the Broncos] were going through," Tebow said. "You don't get many opportunities to have a chance to sign Peyton Manning. What a great quarterback he is."

As always, Tebow was enthusiastic about the future. "Now I'm looking forward to my time as a Jet," he said at the press conference. "I'm very thankful for the opportunity to play for such a great organization. It's my dream and passion to help them out and just be a part of it."

A few days later, NFLShop.com had already started selling green Jets jerseys, printed with the name Tebow and the number 15. New York sports radio shows buzzed with Tebow talk. Newspapers and sports blogs reported

Tim and Mark: Tebow worked out with Mark Sanchez, the Jets starting quarterback, during the summer of 2012.

on Tebow's every move. When he showed up at a New York Yankees baseball game, reporters jumped on the story. Everyone laughed when he said he would change his dog's name from Bronco to Bronx. (The Bronx is a borough of New York City.) Reporters swarmed around Tebow when he practiced with the Jets for the first time in mid-May. They carefully analyzed the body language between him and Mark Sanchez, looking for any signs of tension between the Jets starter and his backup.

There was no stopping Tebowmania. Clearly, it hadn't gone away. It had only moved east.

TIM TEBOW'S REGULAR-SEASON STATISTICS

PASSING STATISTICS

Year	League	Team	Games	Att	Comp	Yards	TD	Int
2006	NCAA	Florida Gators	14	33	22	358	5	1
2007	NCAA	Florida Gators	13	350	234	3,286	32	6
2008	NCAA	Florida Gators	14	298	192	2,746	30	4
2009	NCAA	Florida Gators	14	314	213	2,895	21	5
2010	NFL	Denver Broncos	9	82	41	654	5	3
2011	NFL	Denver Broncos	14	271	126	1,729	12	6

RUSHING STATISTICS

Year	League	Team	Games	Att	Yards	TD
2006	NCAA	Florida Gators	14	89	469	8
2007	NCAA	Florida Gators	13	210	895	23
2008	NCAA	Florida Gators	14	176	673	12
2009	NCAA	Florida Gators	14	217	910	14
2010	NFL	Denver Broncos	9	43	227	6
2011	NFL	Denver Broncos	14	122	660	6

TIMELINE

1987   Tim Tebow is born in the Philippines, where his father runs a religious ministry.

1990   The Tebow family moves from the Philippines back to their hometown of Jacksonville, Florida.

1992   Tim joins his brothers and sisters at the family homeschool. His mom is the teacher. Tim joins a Little League baseball team.

1995   Tim joins a Pop Warner football team.

1998   Tim joins the Jacksonville Tidal Wave, a traveling Little League team.

2001   Tim joins the Trinity Christian Academy junior varsity football team. He plays quarterback, and the team goes undefeated.

2002   Tim joins the Trinity Christian Academy varsity football team. He plays linebacker and tight end.

2003   Tim joins the Nease High football team at quarterback. To meet the requirements for playing at Nease, Tim and his mother move to an apartment in St. Johns County, Florida.

2004   Tim makes his first trip to preach in the Philippines. Tim leads the Nease Panthers to the Florida Division 4A football playoffs. The Panthers lose to St. Augustine in the second playoff round.

2005   Tim, along with ten other top high school quarterbacks, attends the Elite 11 quarterback camp in Southern California. The Nease Panthers win the Florida Division 4A state championships. ESPN airs *Tim Tebow: The Chosen One*, a film about Tim's senior season at Nease. Tim chooses to attend college at the University of Florida.

2006   Tim starts classes at the University of Florida. His team, the Florida Gators, wins the SEC championship and ends the season ranked number two in the United States.

2007   The Gators win the BCS National Championship Game in January. Tim becomes Florida's starting quarterback for the 2007 season. Tim wins the Heisman Trophy, the Davey O'Brien Award, the Maxwell Award, and the Sullivan Award.

2008   The Florida Gators suffer their only loss of the season to the University of Mississippi. Florida wins the SEC title in December.

2009   Florida beats Oklahoma in the BCS championship game in January. Tim graduates from the University of Florida. Tim wins the William V. Campbell Trophy. Florida loses to Alabama in the SEC championship game in December.

2010   Tim launches a charity called the Tim Tebow Foundation. The Denver Broncos pick Tim in the first round of the NFL draft. Tim signs endorsement deals with Nike and Jockey.

2011   Tim writes his autobiography, *Through My Eyes*. Tim becomes the Denver starter in game 6, against Miami. The Tebowing craze begins.

2012   Denver beats Pittsburgh in overtime in the first round of the NFL playoffs. Denver loses to New England in the second round of the playoffs. Denver trades Tim to the New York Jets.

GLOSSARY

bowl game: a postseason football game, common in college football. Most bowl games match up top teams from different college football conferences. The Bowl Championship Series (BCS) game matches up the number one and number two teams in the United States.

dyslexia: a learning disability that makes it difficult for a person to make sense of written words and sentences

endorse: to recommend a business or product, often by appearing in commercials. Many professional athletes endorse athletic shoes, sports drinks, and other products.

eye black: black paint or patches that an athlete wears beneath his or her eyes. The black color absorbs sunlight, cutting down on glare.

fumble: to accidentally drop a football while holding it or running with it

Hail Mary: a long forward pass thrown to the end zone in a last-ditch attempt to score as time runs out in a football game

homeschool: a school set up in a family's home. In most homeschools, parents teach their own children. Some homeschools are made up of children and parents from several families.

line of scrimmage: an imaginary line on a football field that marks the position of the ball at the start of each down

missionary: a person who sets out to teach others about his or her religion

NFL draft: the system by which professional football teams choose eligible college players to join their ranks. A team's win-loss record determines its position in the draft. The team with the worst record gets the first draft pick. The team with the second-worst record gets the next pick and so on.

onside kick: a deliberately short kickoff, designed to give the kicking team a chance of recovering the football. An onside kick must travel at least 10 yards or be touched by a member of the receiving team to be legal.

overtime: an extra period of play, used to determine the winner when two teams are tied at the end of four quarters of football

playoffs: a series of games played after the regular football season. The winner of each playoff game advances to the next round. The loser is eliminated from competition. In the NFL playoffs, the final two teams play each other in the Super Bowl.

sack: to tackle the quarterback behind the line of scrimmage

starter: a quarterback or other player assigned to regularly handle a position, as opposed to a backup, or substitute, player

two-point conversion: a run or completed pass into the end zone instead of the normal extra-point kick. A successful play earns the scoring team two points.

wildcat offense: a special play in which a running back, rather than the quarterback, takes the snap from the center. This "wildcat" quarterback can hand off the ball, run with the ball himself, or pass the ball.

SOURCE NOTES

8-9   Tebowing, "Tebowing," *Tebowing.com*, 2011, http://www.tebowing
.com (April 22, 2012).

12   Tim Tebow, *Through My Eyes*, with Nathan Whitaker (New York: HarperCollins, 2011), 14.

15   Ibid., 41.

15   ESPN, *Tim Tebow: The Chosen One*, television broadcast, December 14, 2005.

17   Ibid.

17   Tebow, *Through My Eyes*, 12.

24   Ibid., 54.

24   ESPN, *Chosen One*.

30   Ibid.

33   Tebow, *Through My Eyes*, 86.

38   Ibid., 101.

41   Ibid., 205–206.

41   Pete Thamel, "A Florida Folk Hero Prepares to Face Reality," *New York Times*, September 1, 2007, http://www.nytimes.com/2007/09/01/sports/ncaafootball/01florida.html (April 22, 2012).

46–47   Tebow, *Through My Eyes*, 128.

47   Pete Thamel, "Behind Tebow, Gators Show They Haven't Lost a Thing," *New York Times*, http://www.nytimes.com/2007/09/16/sports/ncaafootball/16florida.html (April 22, 2012).

51   "Heisman Trophy Winner 2007 Tim Tebow," YouTube video, 1:21, footage of Heisman Trophy ceremony, posted by Raven00714 on December 9, 2007, http://www.youtube.com/watch?v=ElmHXWBiSSM&feature=related (April 22, 2012).

51   "Tim Tebow Speech at Heisman Dinner," YouTube video, 3:24, Tim Tebow speaks at the Heisman Trophy Award Dinner, posted by SangitaShah4 on December 12, 2007, http://www.youtube.com/watch?v=00l2tOcJoPs&feature=related (April 22, 2012).

54   Joshua Robinson, "Tebow Reaches the Top, but He Can Still Climb," *New York Times*, December 10, 2007, http://www.nytimes.com/2007/12/10/sports/ncaafootball/10heisman.html?scp=82&sq=tim+tebow&st=nyt (April 22, 2012).

59   Tebow, *Through My Eyes*, 185.

62 Pete Thamel, "Florida Shows Power and Aims for Title," *New York Times*, December 6, 2008, http://www.nytimes.com/2008/12/07 /sports/ncaafootball/07sec.html?scp=156&sq=tim+tebow&st=nyt (April 22, 2012).

62 Ibid.

65 Pete Thamel, "Florida Raises Another Trophy," *New York Times*, January 9, 2009, http://www.nytimes.com/2009/01/09/sports /ncaafootball/09bcs.html?scp=3&sq=tebow%20oklahoma%20 bcs&st=cse (April 22, 2012).

65 Ibid.

67 Tebow, *Through My Eyes*, 223.

68 Pete Thamel, "Alabama Knocks Florida Off Top," *New York Times*, December 5, 2009, http://www.nytimes.com/2009/12/06/sports /ncaafootball/06sec.html?scp=1&sq=florida%20alabama%20 tebow%202009%20sec&st=cse (April 22, 2012).

70 Mike Klis, *Will to Win: How Tim Tebow and the Denver Broncos Made 2011 a Season to Remember* (Denver: Denver Post, 2012), Kindle edition, chap. 1.

70 Ibid.

70–71 *Tim Tebow: Everything in Between*, DVD (Universal City, CA: Summit Entertainment, 2011).

81 Klis, *Will to Win*, Kindle edition, chap. 1.

90 Ibid.

95 Toni Monkovic, "Tim Tebow's Postgame Comments, and Unclear Future," *New York Times*, January 15, 2012, http://fifthdown.blogs .nytimes.com/2012/01/15/tim-tebows-postgame-comments-and- unclear-future/ (April 22, 2012).

95 Ibid.

95 Judy Battista, "Tebow Stretches Field and Maybe His Limits," *New York Times*, January 10, 2012, http://www.nytimes.com/2012/01/11 /sports/football/tebow-stretches-field-and-maybe-his-limits.html (April 22, 2012).

98 Toni Monkovic, "Tim Tebow Speaks about Trade to Jets," *New York Times*, March 22, 2012, http://fifthdown.blogs.nytimes .com/2012/03/22/tim-tebow-speaks-about-trade-to-jets/ (April 22, 2012).

99 Ibid.

SELECTED BIBLIOGRAPHY

Barry, Dan. "He's a Quarterback, He's a Winner, He's a TV Draw, He's a Verb." *New York Times*, January 13, 2012. http://www.nytimes .com/2012/01/14/sports/football/fascinated-by-tim-tebow-on-more-than-sundays.html?pagewanted=all (April 22, 2012).

Bob Tebow Evangelistic Association. "About the Tebow Family." *BTEA*. 2012. http://www.btea.org/aboutus.asp (April 22, 2012).

Borden, Sam. "Backup to Starter to Phenomenon. Repeat." *New York Times*, March 30, 2012. http://www.nytimes.com/2012/03/31/sports/football /mania-for-tim-tebow-rooted-in-big-moments.html?pagewanted=all (April 22, 2012).

ESPN. *Tim Tebow: The Chosen One*. Television broadcast, December 14, 2005.

Klis, Mike. *Will to Win: How Tim Tebow and the Denver Broncos Made 2011 a Season to Remember*. Denver: Denver Post, 2012.

Sandomir, Richard. "Like Woods Before, Tebow Becomes Must-Watch TV." *New York Times*, January 13, 2012. http://www.nytimes.com/2012/01/14 /sports/football/cbs-sports-ratings-jump-when-tim-tebow-is-playing .html?ref=football (April 22, 2012).

Tebow, Tim. *Through My Eyes*. With Nathan Whitaker. New York: HarperCollins, 2011.

Tim Tebow: Everything in Between. DVD. Universal City, CA: Summit Entertainment, 2011.

FURTHER READING AND WEBSITES

Books

Holmes, Parker. *Tim Tebow*. New York: PowerKids Press, 2012.

Polzer, Tim. *Tim Tebow: Always a Hero*. New York: Scholastic, 2012.

Savage, Jeff. *Mark Sanchez*. Minneapolis: Lerner Publications Company, 2012.

——. *Peyton Manning*. Minneapolis: Lerner Publications Company, 2013.

Stewart, Mark, and Mike Kennedy. *Touchdown! The Power and Precision of Football's Perfect Play*. Minneapolis: Millbrook Press, 2010.

Tebow, Tim. *Through My Eyes: A Quarterback's Journey*. Young Reader's ed. With Nathan Whitaker. New York: Zondervan, 2011.

Torres, John. *Tim Tebow*. Hockessin, DE: Mitchell Lane Publishers, 2012.

Websites

National Football League
http://www.nfl.com
The National Football League website offers the latest news on NFL happenings, links to teams and players, and video highlights, along with scores, schedules, stats, and standings.

New York Jets
http://www.newyorkjets.com
Learn all about Tim Tebow's new team at the Jets' website.

Tebowing
http:www.tebowing.com
Check out this blog to see photos of thousands of people striking Tim's famous pose. You can even submit your own Tebowing photo for publication.

Tim Tebow
http://www.timtebow.com
Tim's own website includes a biography, photos and videos, and messages from Tim's Twitter feed.

Tim Tebow Foundation
http://www.timtebowfoundation.org
Tim began his foundation to help people around the world. You can read about the foundation's activities on this website.

INDEX

PHOTO ACKNOWLEDGMENTS

The images in this book are used with the permission of: © Joe Robbins/Getty Images, p. 1; Joe Skipper/Reuters/Landov, p. 3; AP Photo/Jim Mahoney, p. 4; AP Photo/Eric Bakke, pp. 5, 84, 96; © Al Messerschmidt/Getty Images, p. 7; AP Photo/Kevin Terrell, p. 8; Tebowing.com/Whitehotpix/Zuma Press, p. 9; © Eric L. Wheater/Lonely Planet Images/ Getty Images, p. 10; © Jeff Greenberg/Alamy, p. 14; © Robert Hanashiro/USA TODAY, pp. 16 (top), 22, 36, 42, 52, 63, 74 (top), 78, 92; AP Photo/Scott A. Miller, p. 16 (bottom); © John Coletti/The Image Bank/Getty Images, p. 18; © Severin Schweiger/Cultura/Getty Images, p. 19; AP Photo/NFL Photos, p. 20; Doug Finger/Gainesville Sun/Landov, pp. 21, 46; AP Photo/Times-Courier/Kevin Kilhoffer, p. 23; Tom Hauck/Icon SMI 719/Icon SMI/ Newscom, p. 28; Zuma Press/Newscom, pp. 30, 31; © Joe Murphy/Stringer/Getty Images, p. 32; © Pat Canova/Photolibrary/Getty Images, p. 34; © Patrick Lynch/Alamy, p. 35; © Tom Hauck/Icon SMI/CORBIS, p. 37; © Amy Guip/CORBIS, p. 38; Gary W. Green/ Orlando Sentinel/MCT/Newscom, pp. 39, 48, 71; AP Photo/Phil Sandlin, pp. 40, 43; © Skip Williams/Icon SMI, p. 44; © Andy Lyons/Getty Images, p. 47; © Al Pererira/ WireImage/Getty Images, p. 50; © Cliff Welch/Icon SMI, p. 53; © Kelly Kline/Getty Images, p. 54; © Handout/USA TODAY, p. 56; © Samuel Lewis/Icon SMI, p. 57; © J. Merci/ Getty Images, p. 58; © Stephen M. Dowell/Orlando Sentinel/MCT via Getty Images, p. 60; © Al Diaz/Miami Herald/MCT via Getty Images, p. 61; © Sam Greenwood/Getty Images, p. 66; AP Photo/Stephen Chernin, p. 67; Al Diaz/MCT/Newscom, p. 68; © Chris Szagola/Cal Sport Media/Zuma Press/Icon SMI, p. 72; © Doug Pensinger/Getty Images, pp. 74 (bottom), 86, 90; AP Photo/Ed Andrieski, p. 75; Gary C. Caskey/UPI/Newscom, pp. 76, 82; © Cliff Welch/Icon SMI, p. 79; © Icon SMI, p. 80; © Rick Stewart/Stringer/ Getty Images, p. 85; Allen Eyestone/Zuma Press/Newscom, p. 87; © Jonathan Newton/ The Washington Post via Getty Images, p. 89; © Jeff Gross/Getty Images, p. 91; © Rob Foldy/Icon SMI, p. 94; © Justin Edmonds/Stringer/Getty Images, p. 97; © Jo Stevens/Retna Ltd./CORBIS, p. 98; Leon T. Switzer/Icon SMI BAL/Icon Sports Media/Newscom, p. 99.

Front cover: © Joe Robbins/Getty Images.
Back cover © Robert Deutsch/USA TODAY.

Main body text set in USA TODAY Roman Regular 10.5/15.

ABOUT THE AUTHOR

Stephen G. Gordon was born in Cleveland, Ohio, and graduated from Kent State University. He makes his home in northern New Mexico, where he writes about sports, music, and history.